THINKING ABOUT EDUCATION SERIES
Jonas F. Soltis, *Editor*

This series offers preservice and in-service teachers concise descriptions of contemporary thought about professional ethics, school and society, approaches to teaching, learning theories, and curriculum and aims. Realistic case studies, disputes, and dialogues are included to stimulate thinking about relevant issues in the context of practice.

SCHOOL AND SOCIETY
Walter Feinberg and Jonas F. Soltis

PERSPECTIVES ON LEARNING
D. C. Phillips and Jonas F. Soltis

THE ETHICS OF TEACHING
Kenneth A. Strike and Jonas F. Soltis

CURRICULUM AND AIMS
Decker F. Walker and Jonas F. Soltis

APPROACHES TO TEACHING
Gary D. Fenstermacher and Jonas F. Soltis

APPROACHES
══ TO ══
TEACHING

GARY D. FENSTERMACHER
University of Arizona

JONAS F. SOLTIS
Teachers College, Columbia University

Teachers College, Columbia University
New York and London

Published by Teachers College Press, 1234 Amsterdam Avenue, New York, N.Y. 10027

Library of Congress Cataloging in Publication Data

Fenstermacher, Gary D.
  Approaches to teaching.

  (Thinking about education series)
  Bibliography: p.
  1. Teaching. I. Soltis, Jonas F. II. Title.
III. Series.
LB1025.2.F463 1986   371.1'02   85–30344

ISBN 0-8077-2789-X

Manufactured in the United States of America

91 90 89 88   3 4 5 6

Contents

Acknowledgments

We would like to thank a number of institutions and individuals that have contributed in different ways to the writing of this book and to the completion of the series as a whole. Some of the latter have been mentioned in earlier books in the series. They include Tom Rotell, Lois Patton, and Susan Liddicoat of Teachers College Press. To that list we would now like to add and thank for their sustained efforts on the series' behalf Carole Saltz, who joined the Press as director just as the series got underway; Sandra Pak, who contributed her production expertise; Karen Osborne, who ably served as copy editor; and Mel Berk, who has helped us reach a broad audience. In fact, everyone at the Press has been most supportive. Nancy Soltis also deserves special recognition for her patience, love, and understanding through what sometimes seemed to be the endless process of the nonstop writing of five books. Maybe now the Mystic house will get the attention it deserves. The administration at Teachers College spared the series editor/coauthor from committee work and was most cooperative and generous with the provision of extra computer space and people to help on the project. Once again, Karl Hostetler ably served as research assistant and jack-of-all-trades. He and the following people contributed ideas for the cases and disputes included in chapter 6: Tim Counihan, Susan Moyers, Barbara Reynolds, Janet Skupien, and Michael Weinstock. Fran Simon provided much appreciated word-processing skills. And last but not least we thank our own teachers and colleagues, who have encouraged us to think deeply about teaching.

A Note to the Instructor

This book was designed so that it could be used in a number of ways to suit the purposes and style of the instructor. All or any lesser combination of the five texts in this series can be used together in a basic foundations course. This book or any of the others in this series also can be used singly as the primary text for a full course on its topic, as supplemental reading, or as a source for cases and dialogues to stimulate class discussion. If used as a text in a full course on approaches to teaching, a number of pedagogical options are available.

1. The first five chapters can be treated as you would any text, and then the cases and disputes in chapter 6 can be used to provide materials for class discussions for the remainder of the term. We have found that a case or a dispute can easily produce a good discussion that lasts thirty or more minutes. They raise ethical as well as pedagogical and intellectual issues.
2. We have found that doing a chapter and spending one or two sessions discussing related cases and dialogues is a very effective way to mix the theoretical with the practical. At the beginning of the last chapter, in table 1, we have offered suggestions for specific cases, dialogues, and issues to be discussed as you proceed. We have also made specific suggestions in the text itself.
3. To either of the above approaches could be added class-invented cases, dialogues, or debates that apply theory to practice and raise issues of personal concern about approaches to teaching.
4. Of course, any creative approach to the use of these materials that you can invent will be as good or better than any of our suggestions.

If this book is to be used to treat approaches to teaching as part of a course, then the following options—as well as any you can invent—are available.

1. Spend three to six sessions discussing each of the three approaches dealt with in the substantive chapters and the cases related to them. Table 1 in chapter 6 provides a guide for selecting appropriate cases.
2. Have students read the first five chapters in preparation for a discussion of cases and issues selected by you from chapter 6 for as many sessions as you allot to the study of approaches to teaching.
3. Have students read the text without discussing any of the cases and disputes. This option misses a great opportunity to stimulate student thinking by using the case method approach.

If you have not taught using the case method before, the following suggestions may be of some help.

1. It is important to establish a good climate for discussion, one in which individuals feel free to express their views openly without fear of ridicule and also feel free to challenge the honest views of others with reasonable arguments and genuine alternatives.
2. Good group discussions are facilitated by asking students to read cases and sketch their answers to case problems before class so a discussion can start with some forethought and direction.
3. Some of our cases appear in more than one book in this series. Using them will allow you to demonstrate the multidimensionality of real-life situations in which different issues come to light when different interests are operative and different questions are asked.
4. Pedagogically, as a discussion leader it is useful to summarize along the way, to help students see the ideas at issue, to bring in relevant theoretical knowledge, and to guide discussions to some reasonable conclusion, however firm or tentative.
5. And remember, students can learn worthwhile things even when their instructor is not talking.

We trust you will find this book to be a versatile pedagogical tool useful in getting students not only to learn about basic philosophical approaches to teaching, but also to think about them as they make practical applications and face personal, pedagogical, and moral educational issues.

APPROACHES TO TEACHING

Chapter 1

The Teacher As . . .

This is a book about different approaches to teaching. In it we want to stimulate you to think about some basic ways to conceive of the role of the teacher. We believe that how you approach your teaching will have a great effect on what you do as a teacher. To help you see what we mean, consider some of the analogies often used to characterize teaching and try to imagine what you might do as a teacher if you believed them literally. No one takes them literally, of course, but if you did, you might approach teaching in very different ways. Think about the teacher as

> *Gardener:* Tending to the development and nurturance of young grow-
> ing things. Imagine an art lesson using this approach.
> *Potter:* Shaping formless clay into useful objects. Imagine the same art
> lesson. Would using this approach make it different?
> *Midwife:* Assisting in the birth of ideas and knowledge. Imagine a
> math lesson using this approach.
> *Provisioner:* Providing a store of knowledge and skills needed for the
> journey of life. Imagine the same math lesson based on this per-
> spective.

You might want to stop here and sketch out your ideas of what these different approaches to teaching might be like in these lessons before going on to see how we imagined them.

An Art Lesson

It was spring. Mrs. Gardner never ceased to be touched by the children's spontaneous gifts of fists full of dandelions and, occasionally, a pilfered tulip or daffodil. Painting flowers just had to be the art lesson today! She pulled from her file folder a sample of flower paintings her students had done over the years and hung them around the room. After her aides distributed the painting materials, Mrs. Gardner told the children to look at the paintings but also to try to remember what the flowers they had seen on the way to school looked like and how they made them feel; then to try to paint a bouquet to please someone at home. As the children worked, Mrs. Gardner moved among them encouraging the reticent, praising the productive, helping those who had problems, and drawing the children's attention to the beautiful variety of colors and flowers that were growing on all their papers.

Mr. Potter, in the next room, had also decided it was a good time to give his very successful flower painting lesson. He knew the children had not yet mastered the mixing of colors and this lesson would help them form that skill. Because tulips were in bloom around town, it was an ideal time to distribute the tulip templates for the children to use to trace four flowers on their papers. This would also strengthen eye-hand coordination and give them all some immediate reinforcement of success. Each table had only three paint pots: red, yellow, and blue. Mr. Potter told the class that they were going to learn to do something they had not done before—create colors. The class was excited. He had them watch as he mixed a little red paint with yellow on his paper palette. The magic of orange was greeted with a chorus of "Ooooh!" The same squeal came with blue and red making purple. Then, after painting his four flowers red, yellow, orange, and purple, Mr. Potter painted a blue stem on each. As the children began to object, he covered the blue paint with yellow, thus making green and raising one last chorus of "Ooooh!" "Now try it yourselves," Mr. Potter said, "and remember, you can make your own colors if you ever need to."

A Math Lesson

When Mrs. Middleweiss asked if anyone had ever painted a room at home, many hands shot in the air. But when she asked how you could know how much paint to buy, only Karl braved a guess. Karl said, "The label on the paint can tells you how many square feet a gallon will cover and so you just figure it out." "But how?" she asked the class. "What is a square foot anyway, and how do you count square feet in a room?" The problem of defining square feet was quickly settled, and the class decided to follow Juanita's suggestion that they try a picture-solution approach on the blackboard by drawing a representative wall of a room. Mary volunteered, "We need to know the measurements first," and Mrs. Middleweiss made the wall 8 feet high and 10 feet wide. Then Paul suggested drawing square feet on the wall and counting them. Everybody thought that was a good idea, and it was done. They counted 80 squares. Karl noticed something: 8 times 10 is 80. He asked to try something. He added 2 more feet to the drawing, filled in the squares, counted 96, and then announced to the class that he had found an easier way—multiply height by base! Mrs. Middleweiss agreed that it was a good strategy and then complicated the picture by putting a 2-foot by 4-foot window in the wall. Hands shot up. "Subtract 8 square feet from 96 and you get 88!" a number of children shouted in unison. "Unless you're going to paint the windows," someone added *sub voce*. The problem of the amount of paint needed was soon settled, and the children had learned the general idea of how to find the area of a rectangle.

Mr. Provider, the math teacher next door to Mrs. Middleweiss, also prided himself on making abstract math principles sufficiently concrete and practical that his students could easily learn them and see their use in everyday life. Today he was going to cover ways to compute areas of plane surfaces bounded by straight lines. He wanted at least to get through rectangular area ($A = bh$), but if there was time, he would like to cover $A = \frac{1}{2} bh$ for triangles, too. He began by showing students how much of their everyday world was made up of rectangles—in rooms, windows, and doors; in the yard, tennis court, and football field; and so forth. He noted that such ordinary tasks as painting rooms, curtaining windows, and seeding yards required that we know how much area we were dealing with so we could get the right amount of paint, fabric, or seed. "Fortunately," Mr. Provider added, "there is a simple formula that will help us figure this area. It is base times height." He did a number of examples of yards, tennis courts, and windows on the board until he was sure his students had the basic idea. Mr. Provider first had Andrew figure the area of a 10-foot by 8-foot wall without a window; he then added the same window that had been used to find curtain area in the earlier example. This made it easy for the class to see that $A = bh$ should be modified by subtracting any subarea within the total area that was not to be treated in the same way as the rest of A. Mr. Provider wrote his version of this new formula on the board [$A = bh (-a)$], and then he added a pitched roofline triangle to the wall to move the class along to consider the next formula he wanted to present before the period ended.

These cases should make it clear that not only are there different ways to teach the same things (and probably very effectively), but also that a teacher's approach, his or her general conception of the teacher's role, plays an important part in *how* one teaches. In this book, we are going to help you explore and think about three very basic approaches to teaching. For convenience, we have named them the "executive," the "therapist," and the "liberationist" approaches, although they go by many names. Each has its historical roots as well as its contemporary research and scholarly support structure. But most important, each can give you a way to think about, diagnose, and prescribe what you as a teacher should do.

You must remember, however, that these approaches are *conceptions* of teaching. They are ideas about what teaching is and should be. As such, they are products of the human mind and not some immutable reflection of the way the world really is. As such, they are also open to appraisal and criticism, adoption, rejection, or modification. They are three different perspectives that contemporary educators have used to conceive of the activities of teaching in ways that they think will help us do it better.

Three Approaches to Teaching

The executive approach views the teacher as an executor, a person charged with bringing about certain learnings, using the best skills and techniques available. Contemporary research on the effects of teaching and learning is very important to this approach. It provides the teacher with techniques and understandings to use in the management of the classroom and the production of learning. Our imaginary Mr. Potter and Mr. Provider may have been using this approach.

The therapist approach views the teacher as an empathetic person charged with helping individuals grow personally and reach a high level of self-actualization, understanding, and acceptance. Psychotherapy, humanistic psychology, and existential philosophy underwrite this view, which focuses on students' developing their own selves as authentic persons through personally meaningful educational experiences. Mrs. Gardner may have been using this approach.

The liberationist approach views the teacher as a liberator, a freer of the individual's mind and a developer of well-rounded, autonomous, rational, and moral human beings. Mrs. Middleweiss may have been using it. The classical idea of a liberal education underwrites the contemporary mainstream version of this approach, and it is the one we will focus on in this book.[1]

We hope you can now see that there is much to learn and think about regarding approaches to teaching. Of course, one can teach without thinking about one's approach toward teaching just as one can be a lover or parent without giving much thought to the meaning of love or the duties and responsibilities of parenting. But we believe that professional teachers only become professionals when they reflect on and choose a stance toward their calling that guides and sustains them in their important work of educating persons. We also believe that, in this instance, knowledge is power. Knowing about different approaches to teaching will give you the power to choose ways to teach that will help you achieve the highest goals of one of the noblest of professions, helping individuals to become full-fledged persons. Moreover, understanding different approaches offers ways to think about what one is doing and what relation there is between what one intends as a teacher and what one actually does with learners. This is part of being a responsible, reflective, committed educator.

This may sound as if we will be asking you to choose one stance of the three we treat. As a matter of fact, we will be doing the opposite. We will be arguing that each approach contains within it values and purposes that are useful and appropriate in certain teaching situations, as well as being morally preferable in some instances. We may not convince you. In fact, we will display these approaches as basically incompatible and in conflict with each other. Therefore, you may see overriding reasons for adopting one stance over another. You would not be alone in that regard. You may argue for the consistency, correctness, or moral superiority of one position. All we will ask you to do regarding our position is to think seriously about the strengths and weaknesses of these approaches, about their appropriateness for dealing with human beings, and about your own commitments as an educator. However you end up, it will be *your* way and *your* view thoughtfully and deliberately chosen; and that is our goal as we encourage you to think about various approaches to teaching.

We end this book with a chapter of cases and disputes that we hope you will use selectively, as you go through each chapter, to focus and stimulate your thinking about important issues and applications of these basic approaches to teaching. But before going on to examine each of the three approaches treated in this book, or to suggest cases in chapter 6 that are relevant to this introduction, there are a few other important ways of thinking about teaching that need preliminary consideration.

Educating Persons

In our examples of the art and math lessons, we tried to help you see that the same lessons could be taught using different approaches. What a teacher thinks teaching is, be it like gardening, potting, midwifing, or providing (or like management, therapy, or liberation), determines the direction, tone, and style of the teacher. But something else also has a great influence on how teachers teach: their conception of what they would like their students eventually to become. What kinds of persons are good, happy, knowledgeable, productive persons, and how can education assist students in the process of becoming educated persons?

To help us try to answer this question, imagine that upon becoming an educated person individuals were issued an E-P card, a certificate about the size of a credit card. Across the top, in large, bold letters (just like the name of the bank on a credit card) is written **Educated Person**. What would entitle human beings to an E-P card? What would be its requirements? In order to be able to answer these questions (and perhaps to know if you can qualify for such a card yourself), you would need to be able to specify what an educated person is. That should not be too much of a problem. "An educated person is someone who has learned the basics: reading, writing, and arithmetic. . . . No, you need more than that. You need to graduate from high school. . . . No, college. . . . Wait a minute; some people graduate from high school and even from college without being very well educated. . . . Perhaps you also need to. . . . Oh, oh." Not quite so easy as it might at first seem! Let us start again.

You might say an educated person simply is anyone who graduates from some agreed upon institution of education, be it elementary school, high school, or college. That is all it takes to qualify. Then all would get E-P cards at graduation, just like everyone now gets diplomas. But we know some people with diplomas are not really educated and some who never got their diplomas have managed to educate themselves. So you might want to say that being an educated person requires more than just putting in time in an educational institution and graduating. You might think that an educated person should be one who has attained the acceptable level of knowledge and skill required for taking on the responsibilities of adulthood. But maybe even that is not enough. Perhaps being an educated person should also require knowledge of the classics, appreciation of art and music, and possession of a critical mind. Perhaps it should even require becoming a morally responsible human being. Or it might require even more than that. What do you think? What is your conception of an educated person?

Notice what is happening with these specifications. They begin at a very basic, no-nonsense level—an educated person is a graduate from some specified educational institution—and move all the way toward some grand conception of a full-fledged Educated Person. The definition shifts from being minimally descriptive to being increasingly prescriptive; from telling us what an educated person is in some ordinary sense, to telling us what one ought to be if one is to be considered a fully educated person in some ideal sense. As a definition like this one of "educated person" shifts in this way, philosophers say it is becoming more normative in character. *Normative* means evaluative, specifying desirable norms, characteristics, or standards. The idea of the normative is important, for it is almost impossible to talk about education and teaching without introducing normative value considerations. Educating is a normative activity directed at helping individuals develop into some image of what it means to be a full-fledged human being. More on this later as we discuss the different approaches and their different normative assumptions and implications. Let us get back to the E-P card.

One's eligibility for the card depends a great deal on the full meaning of "educated person." If an educated person is simply a graduate, then one only needs to attend school and achieve minimal standards to qualify for the card; everyone would get one at graduation. If, on the other hand, one needs to acquire certain characteristics to be fully recognized as an educated person, then some qualifying criteria must be met before obtaining the card. To understand what this means, let us simplify things and suppose that there were only four basic qualifying criteria in a certain society for eligibility to educated personhood. In that society, before an E-P card can be issued to anyone, he or she must be able to (1) read and demonstrate comprehension of ordinary, everyday reading material, (2) write and speak cogently and clearly, (3) make ordinary calculations needed in everyday life, and (4) be familiar with the laws and the constitution of the nation in which the individual lives.

If these four items were criteria for the card, you would know a lot more about a person who carried it than if merely being a graduate of some school was the sole criterion for the card. As a matter of fact, you might like these qualifying criteria so much that you think *everyone* minimally should meet them in the society in which you live, no matter what kind of school they attend or whether they graduate. After all, to be a good and productive citizen one should have to be verbally and mathematically literate, capable of being a self-sustaining, contributing member of society, and aware of the basic values, rights, and obligations of being a citizen.

In every society some form of education is required of everyone to prepare them to play their role as educated persons. To meet the far-reaching demand for the education of all, schools are established, publicly supported, and mandated as places for the next generation to go to obtain the requisite education. In this way, in all but the most elemental societies, schools are where people go to obtain their Educated-Person cards.

Therefore, what a society determines an educated person to be—that is, what criteria it determines must be met before the E-P card is issued—also influences to a considerable degree what teachers do in their classrooms. If society says that the card is issued to those who can read, write, and calculate, that might influence the teacher's approach in one way. If society favors emotional well-being, mental health, and happiness over reading, writing, and calculation, then the teacher's approach is likely to be different. One's approach and one's conception of an educated person are tied together tightly.

A Helpful Formula

As we examine the several approaches to teaching in this book, it will be helpful to have a device to keep the significant features of each approach from being lost in the details of the discussion. We have already hinted at the complexity of the factors involved. In our own teaching about these approaches, we have found that a short formula will do the trick. It goes like this: $T\phi Sxy$. The symbol between the T and the S is the Greek letter *phi*. It designates an action. The formula is read as follows: The *teacher* (T) *teaches* (ϕ) the *student* (S) some *content* (x) in order to attain some *purpose* (y). This seemingly simple device carries enormous complexities, problems, issues, and insights in its wake.

Take, for example, the x or content part of the formula. Not only does the x designate certain subject areas, such as literature, mathematics, or history, it also symbolizes different aspects of the content to be acquired—as facts, as skills, as understandings, as beliefs, as sentiments, or even as traits of character. For example, suppose you are teaching chemistry and have the students do a distillation experiment. In addition to using this exercise to teach about states and phases (e.g., liquid, solid, gas), which is something (x_1) you want the students to *know about*, you also teach them (x_2) *how to* set up a distillation apparatus. Setting up the distillation apparatus is something you want the students to learn to be able *to do*; it is a skill, and as such is a kind of capability different from the knowledge they have about phases and states. Thus the meaning of x can vary and be multiple. It might designate any number of different kinds of student outcomes, and different approaches may stress different sets of these. For the time being, there is no need to get caught up in any of the complexities. Indeed, the point of the formula is to reduce the apparent complexity of the different approaches to teaching as we examine each one in depth. Here is another illustration of how the formula works.

Take the y symbol designating purpose in our formula. To what end (y) does the teacher engage the student in the study of some content (x)? We will examine three major purposes in this book. The first is to acquire specified knowledge, the second is to become an authentic person, and the third is to liberate the mind. You will see how a change in y can alter ϕ and x dramatically. When the teacher undertakes teaching (ϕ) with the purpose of preparing the students to learn something in particular ($y =$ executive purpose), then the teacher's approach to the student and to the content is very different from when the teacher sets out to free the mind of the student ($y =$ liberationist purpose) or to develop the self ($y =$ therapist purpose). For example, imagine a teacher of English literature using the executive approach. He or she probably would structure the course and individual lessons in ways designed to prepare students to go on to take more advanced courses in English literature and perhaps eventually to become specialists in English literature. Emphasis would be on covering the field and gaining specific knowledge.

Imagine another teacher using the liberationist approach. He or she might teach students English literature with the primary intention of getting them to think about aspects of human nature and human emotions not likely to be encountered in their everyday experiences and helping them to see and understand other ways of thinking about and perceiving the world. This teacher believes that, just as travel broadens the mind, so does learning about things beyond one's immediate ken. It frees one from the narrowness of one's own small world.

Imagine a third teacher using the therapist approach. He or she might use literature to help students see into their own souls, to help them recognize their own depths of feeling and being in ways they might not have been able to articulate before. Becoming educated for this teacher is coming to know and forming one's self authentically. Teaching is helping people become their real selves.

Which literature teacher would you rather have? Do you already have a predisposition toward one of these approaches? Before going on to the next chapter, in which we will more fully examine the executive approach, you may want to look in chapter 6 at the case "Grading Policies" and at the dispute over what it really means to be "An Educated Person." This will give you a chance to examine your own predispositions toward these approaches and the concept of Educated Person before you begin a more rigorous study of these important issues. There is also a case in chapter 6 called "School and Approach Mismatch" that raises another problem with choosing your own approach. You will see that there is much to think about in this regard.

Chapter 2

The Executive Approach

Classrooms are complex places. Often twenty-five to thirty-five children are contained in a rather tight space, along with one or two adults. There is a great deal going on. The children are there because they are supposed to be there, and the teachers are trying to engage their students in the study of whatever content is prescribed. The complexity of classrooms, when joined with the demand that certain things take place there, means that they must in some way be managed.

Managing a Classroom

How do you manage a classroom? Think about it. You have to engage all the students in academic work of some sort. To do that, you have to determine what they are to be taught (curriculum guides might help here). Then you must figure out whether the students who are in *your* classroom are able (ready) to learn what is prescribed for them. After you have diagnosed the students to determine their readiness for the material you want to present, you may find that they are not quite up to it. You may have to revise the material, adapting it to make it accessible to your students. Once you have the material ready, you have to figure out how to get it across. What motivational devices might be used to interest the students and keep them engaged? What classroom structure best contributes to successful learning—small groups, large groups, whole-class instruction, or independent learning?

And this is only the *planning* stage. After you figure out what is to be done, then you must do it. No matter how well you plan, events will occur that cause you to veer from your plan. In the course of teaching, you are constantly making decisions about the students, the material, and the overall success or failure of your efforts. You probably will revise your plan many times while on your feet teaching the lesson. Then after you teach it, you may follow up with an evaluation, only to find that a mere six out of twenty-eight students understood more than half of what you taught. Now you have to reteach the unit, but you are stymied about how to reconstruct it so that most of the students will understand it.

All this complexity requires careful planning, action carried out on the basis of the plan (although with many revisions en route), then follow-up evaluation, revised plans, and another instructional effort. These are the kinds of things that executives do. They plan, execute the plan, appraise their effort, then revise and act again. Executives, by and large, manage people and resources. They make decisions about what people will do, when they will do it, how long it is likely to take, and what standard of performance determines whether to move on to the next task or repeat the old one.

Until recently very little thought was given to the teacher as an executive. On the contrary, teachers were thought simply to be experts in the subjects they taught, while students were willing participants in the teaching of these subjects. The task of teaching seemed fairly straightforward: Just get the youngsters together, present them with a well-constructed lesson, and you could go home knowing that you did a day's work well. This view prevailed for a good part of the last century and most of this one. Then researchers began studying actual classroom settings. They found them far more complex than the folk wisdom of the time had led most people to believe. And they found teachers engaged in more complex and sophisticated endeavors than they had traditionally been given credit for.

As our understanding of the complexity of the classroom situation emerged from research on teaching, it became clear that teachers were more than subject-matter experts with interesting gimmicks for getting that subject matter across to their students. What the researchers found were teachers who managed classroom aides, dealt with angry parents, handled school administrators who sometimes intervened in classrooms in unhelpful ways, coped with irrelevant or inappropriate textbooks and supplementary materials, and spent great amounts of time complying with policy mandates from local, state, and federal regulations; all this, *plus* teaching the students in their classes.

Not surprisingly, researchers were impressed that teachers faced all these tasks and pressures and handled them with varying degrees of success. Some researchers (particularly David Berliner[1]) found the metaphor of the executive to be an accurate and helpful one to use in understanding the work of a teacher. However, it was not simply the pressure and complexity of the classroom that made the executive metaphor appealing. Something else was emerging from the studies of teachers. It seems that effective teaching might be analyzed into a discrete set of generic, or common, skills. That is, regardless of the grade level, the nature of the students, the subject matter, or the culture of the school, certain instructional practices seemed to be regularly associated with gains in student achievement, while other instructional practices appeared unrelated to student mastery of content. Discrete executive skills for teaching could be identified.

For example, the practice of acting friendly with the class—discussing ballgames, the latest national news, and the hot gossip around school—is *not* a practice associated with gains in student learning. That may not seem much of a surprise to you, but you would be amazed at how much time many teachers spend in this kind of academically irrelevant activity. And though it may not be news to you that students are not learning science when a teacher is talking about a football game, incidents such as these alerted researchers to the importance of the time variable in student learning. They rediscovered a very simple idea: By and large, students learn what they study, and how much they learn is in large measure determined by how much time they are engaged in that study.

Not surprising, is it? What is surprising is the way schools and teachers dealt with time. Consider a distinction that comes from one of the most famous of the instructional time studies, the Beginning Teacher Evaluation Study (BTES).[2] BTES researchers distinguished between allocated time and engaged time. Allocated time is how much time a teacher or school sets aside for the study of some subject. Engaged time is the time a *given student* actually works at the subject. What the researchers found is that elementary schools and teachers varied widely in allocated time for the different subjects. Some teachers would, for example, allocate forty-five minutes a day to math, while others would allocate thirty minutes; some would allocate thirty-five minutes to science, others would hardly touch science study; some teachers always devoted forty to fifty minutes a day to social studies, while others would allocate zero to fifteen minutes to it some days and sixty to ninety minutes on other days.

Time on Task

Clearly the amount of time allocated to a subject makes a tremendous difference in students' opportunity to learn it. If the teacher does not spend much time with mathematics, then it is not surprising that his students fare poorly on math exams. However, this variation in allocated time was not the big surprise of the research on instructional time. The big surprise was in engaged time. By focusing on selected students in a classroom, the researchers clocked the amount of time these target students were engaged in the assigned activity, or "on-task." What they found was that, even though a teacher might *allocate* fifty minutes to math, a student might be on-task only seven or eight of that fifty minutes! The engaged time for the student was less than 20 percent of the allocated time.

Consider the impact of this finding. If, in general, students learn subject content only if they study it (you do not learn what you do not study), and the amount of that learning is directly related to the amount of time spent studying (the more you study the more you learn, generally speaking), then in order to learn something well it is necessary to spend a fair amount of time with it. However, by looking at selected students, it was found that some students spent only seven out of fifty minutes on the actual academic task. How could this happen? It is far easier to slip up than you might think. Consider this example.

You set aside fifty minutes for the math unit. It begins right after recess, which ends at 10:35 A.M. The students do not get back at the same time, so you wait until they are all in their seats. Time: 10:39. There are some announcements and a few things you want them to know about activities this afternoon and later this week. Time: 10:41. There is an outburst in the back of the room. You settle that. Time: 10:42. You start the math lesson with some directions about a task you want everybody to do in his or her workbook, saying that they should take five minutes for this assignment and then the whole class will discuss it. You spend some time explaining how you want students to do the task. These instructions are not teaching them anything about math, only about how to complete the workbook pages. Time: 10:46. Eleven minutes gone and no math activity has occurred yet.

At last the students are working in the books. It so happens that Harry, however, did not really understand your instructions. Because he is rather shy, he does not raise his hand for help. It is 10:49 before you notice him doodling on the margin of the book. You walk back to his desk and clear up the confusion; he begins to work fifteen minutes after the scheduled beginning of the math period. Within two minutes, he is confused. He puzzles over the difficulty for a while, then stops working. It is 10:53 and Harry is off-task. You are busy with the other students, so do not notice his problem. He is too embarrassed to ask for help again, especially since you were somewhat exasperated with him the time before. He waits until you start class discussion to learn the solution to the problem that threw him off. You are a little late getting the group started in discussion. It is 10:58 before the discussion begins.

Harry goes back on-task at the beginning of the discussion and stays with you for the duration of the discussion, which concludes at 11:11. Thus he was on-task for thirteen minutes of the discussion plus two minutes during the workbook exercise. Thirty-six minutes of allocated time have elapsed, and Harry has accumulated fifteen minutes of engaged time. You have a chance to increase the percentage of Harry's engaged time by insuring that the remaining fourteen minutes of allocated time are constructed so that Harry can be actively involved in the content of the lesson. But that does not happen because you look at the clock, note that it is 11:11 and that the period is scheduled to end at 11:25, and conclude that it is not worthwhile for you to begin another unit with so little time remaining. So you assign the students to another activity in their workbooks in order to fill the remaining time. Harry goes along just fine for three more minutes, then becomes stumped again. You are not monitoring student seatwork, however, so you do not see him gazing out the window. You have an attendance report that must be filed before 11:30, so you take these few minutes to complete it. At 11:25 you call the math period to a halt. Harry has been on-task in the study of math for eighteen of the fifty minutes, just about 35 percent of the available time.

Features of This Approach

Researchers have found that there are many ways for teachers to increase the time that students are engaged. These skills for managing learning time are considered generic teaching skills because they appear to be unrelated to student background characteristics like race or home environment, to the subject matter taught, or to the nature of the school setting. The teacher is seen as manager of classroom time, as one who makes decisions about the way student time will be used in the classroom. Time, however, is not the only aspect of the executive approach to teaching (although it has become one of the most important dimensions). Matching curriculum and evaluation is another aspect, wherein attention is given to the nature of what is taught in relation to what is assessed by tests. It sometimes turns out that students score poorly on tests, not because they failed to master what was taught, but because they were never taught what the tests measured. The teacher who is a good executive will seek a clear match between what is taught and what is assessed by tests.

Another aspect of the executive approach is known as opportunity to learn—giving students the chance to learn what is being taught. Sometimes teachers embark on complex topics or ideas but allow too little opportunity for students to become involved in these topics to the extent that the topics demand. The material is covered too quickly, without adequate background preparation, or is misrepresented in order to cover it in the short time allowed. Any of these factors denies the student adequate opportunity to learn the material.

There is an interesting facet to all these features of the executive approach to teaching. They all place a high premium on student learning. What is so strange about that? Is not student learning what schools and teachers are all about? Well, yes . . . in a way. The difficulty arises when we ask what the students are learning and how that learning is assessed. Let us look at the assessment issue for a moment. The formula $(T\phi Sxy)$ discussed in the last chapter will help here.

Recall that the x stands for the content to be learned. The teacher strongly disposed toward the executive approach views x as specific facts, ideas, topics, or perspectives to be gotten into the heads of the learners. The executive skills we looked at above are the means for moving this specified knowledge from its classroom source (text, supplementary material, lectures, and so forth) to its destination (the student's mind). Remember that ϕ in $T\phi Sxy$? It is the activity of teaching. In this case, ϕ is teaching that is characterized by extensive use of executive skills, including time-management techniques, matching content taught to what the tests measure, and establishing sufficient opportunity to learn.

The purpose (y) of this activity is that students will acquire the specific knowledge communicated by the teacher. Thus, in the executive approach to teaching, $T\phi Sxy$ can be interpreted as follows: The teacher (T) uses certain organizational and management skills (ϕ) to impart to students (S) specific facts, concepts, skills, and ideas (x) so that these students are most likely to acquire and retain this specified knowledge (y). This conception of teaching emphasizes quite direct connections between what the teacher does and what the student learns. Indeed, the form of research used to study the executive approach to teaching is often called "process–product research." The process is the teacher's activity (ϕ), while the product is the student's mastery of what is taught (y). The literature about this form of teaching is often referred to as the "teacher-effectiveness" literature, because so much stress is placed on the effectiveness of the classroom teacher.

Criticisms

If you pursue the assumptions and implications of the executive approach to teaching, certain disturbing things turn up. The teacher seems like the manager of a kind of production line, where students enter the factory as raw material and are somehow "assembled" as persons (they earn their Educated-Person card by successfully acquiring the specified knowledge dispensed at school). The teacher is not so much an actual part of the process as a manager of it. The teacher is not, it seems, "inside" the process of teaching and learning but "outside," where he or she regulates the content and the activities of the learner. Indeed, some critics have viewed the time-management aspects of the executive approach as akin to an oarmaster on an ancient slave ship—the one who stands, beating a large drum, to keep the rowers on-task.

These characterizations of the executive approach—as factory manager, production-line supervisor, or slave-ship oarmaster—offend our sensibilities about education. Most of us do not like to think about children, learning, school, and teaching along the same lines as factories or slave ships. Yet the executive approach invites comparison to such things. It stresses attention to task, performance of duty, achievement results, and accountability for failure to produce. The executive approach seems to disregard parts of education that many think are of utmost importance, such as the nature and interests of individual students, the special characteristics of different subject matters, and the varying demands that differences in geography, economics, and culture make on what takes place in school.

What do you think? Are you ready to abandon this approach as unfaithful to your ideals of education? Are you disappointed that what seemed a useful way to approach teaching turns out to have such unsavory features? Or will you hold on to this approach in the belief that its value outweighs its faults? What are the arguments for holding on to it? Let us take a look.

In the introductory chapter you met Mr. Provider, the math teacher who wanted his students to learn to compute surface area. Imagine that you are Mr. P. You want students to master the computation of plane surfaces bounded by straight lines. You want them to master the appropriate formula ($A = bh$) and be able to apply this formula correctly. You have a clear idea of the x you want to get across. What about the ϕ? How are you going to teach all those S's this x? Why not use the executive approach? It seems ideally suited to this outcome. In fact, it appears as if you would be a fool not to approach this teaching task according to the executive approach. Bring the class together right away, discuss the objective of this lesson, teach the lesson clearly and without exceeding the students' ability to comprehend you, assign seatwork so that students can practice what you are teaching them, monitor their seatwork closely, follow up with a clarification presentation, check for understanding, then test to determine whether they mastered the content. Could there be any better way?

Maybe. Think about some things that are missing from this little scenario. Do the students have any interest in computing the surface area? Are they able to perceive a value or use for this knowledge? Is there a better way to introduce this material? Will what they learn from Mr. P. enhance their understanding of mathematics? Will any of them ever wonder how to compute areas bounded by curved lines? Does Mr. P. care very much about this lesson (do you?), or is he teaching it because this is what is next in the textbook that the school district has adopted? If you want some answers to these questions, do not look to the executive approach. This approach deals primarily with generic skills of teaching, skills that are independent of the content taught, the context in which teaching occurs, and the backgrounds of the students and teachers.

Teacher Effectiveness

If the executive approach does not account for content, context, or culture, what is its value? We have already looked at one answer to this question. Its value is that it provides a very clear, straightforward means to move some specified knowledge from a source (for example, a book, teacher, or film) to the mind of the learner. Indeed, if followed with care, the executive approach increases the probability that more of the students will learn more of the content than would otherwise be the case. As one prominent researcher put it, "teacher effectiveness refers to the ability of a classroom teacher to produce higher than predicted gains on standardized achievement tests."[3] Why is it important that x be moved from source to student as efficiently and effectively as possible? Just a bit of recent history answers this question and throws a great deal of light on the executive approach to teaching.

The school-as-factory analogy has been around for a long time in American education, and so has the doctrine that schools ought to be efficient. Both these ideas emerged late in the last century. But the notion that an effective teacher is one who produces higher-than-predicted gains in student achievement (as measured by standardized tests) is an idea barely past the age of majority. It got its start in the stimulus-response-reward psychology of Edward L. Thorndike in the early twentieth century and gained legitimacy by midcentury in the work on operant conditioning by the famous behavioral psychologist B. F. Skinner. In 1954, in a paper suggestively entitled "The Science of Learning and the Art of Teaching," Skinner contended that "the whole process of becoming competent in any field must be divided into a very large number of very small steps, and reinforcement [i.e., reward] must be contingent upon the accomplishment of each step."[4] Ten years later he stated the point even more boldly: "The application of operant conditioning to education is simple and direct. Teaching is the arrangement of contingencies of reinforcement under which students learn."[5] In simple terms, teachers could bring about the learning they sought from students by knowing precisely when and how to reward students for behaviors that increasingly approximated the goals set for them.

Skinner's contentions about teaching and learning set the stage for two things. First, they encouraged many educators to strip away much of the mystique about teaching as an ineffable human activity. Second, they led educational researchers to draw a tighter loop around the interaction between teacher and learner. The notion of teaching as stimulus, or cause, and learning as response, or effect, enabled researchers to focus exclusively on these two behaviors, without becoming sidetracked by the family backgrounds of students, their life histories, or the particular subject matter to be learned. Skinner's work had a powerful effect on the conceptions that many of us have about teaching and learning, and how the former affects the latter.

These conceptions might not have influenced the actual practice of education too extensively, save for some events taking place in the political and economic sectors of our society at the time. Following the *Brown* versus *Board of Education* decision in 1954, the federal government made ever-increasing commitments to schooling as an instrument for the eradication of poverty and ignorance among racial and ethnic minorities. These commitments reached a very high intensity in the mid-sixties with President Lyndon Johnson's Great Society programs, such as Head Start, Follow Through, and Parent-Child Centers. As more and more dollars were channeled into education, policy makers became increasingly curious about how the money was being spent and whether it was actually helping the students for whom it was targeted.

The Coleman Report

If, perchance, you were not an active follower of the news in the mid-sixties, you may not know that, as part of the Civil Rights Act of 1964, Congress mandated a study of equal educational opportunity among various racial and ethnic groups. This study was directed by James Coleman and is most frequently referred to as the Coleman Report.[6] Using a massive sample of 600,000 students, 60,000 teachers, and 4,000 schools, Coleman found that the amount of money spent on schools did not seem to make much difference in the achievement of those who attended them. He found that different racial groups attended different schools, that the physical differences among these schools were not all that great, that such differences in facilities and professional personnel as he could find did not make much difference in what students accomplished, and that white students often learned far more in their schools than students belonging to other racial and ethnic groups learned in theirs.

That last sentence says a great deal. You might want to read it again. According to Coleman, equality of educational achievement was not obtained by making educational facilities equal. What made an educational difference was the background of the students (particularly parents' income and educational levels). Coleman's data indicated that student peers had a far stronger influence on educational attainment (or lack of it) than the quality of the school's physical facilities, the richness of its curriculum, or the preparation of its teachers. These findings were devastating for educators, who thought that they and their schools had a dramatic impact on student learning.

To understand exactly what is going on here, we have to look at the notion of variance in student achievement. We know, for example, that in 1964 blacks and whites, as groups, varied dramatically in what they learned in school. Once you accept that fact, then the question centers on what accounts for this large variation in achievement. Coleman argued that family background and peer influence accounted for most of the variance and that schools and teachers had little effect on the variance. That was the conclusion that bothered educators, cast doubt on Great Society programs, and led those who controlled educational dollars to look harder at how they were being spent.

After the initial shock of the Coleman Report, researchers began to find flaws in it. The first questions were about the statistics used to analyze the data, then about the design of the study, and, inevitably, about the validity of the conclusions. New research programs were begun, programs that were particularly pointed at finding out whether Coleman was correct.

Research on Teaching

The behaviorists' cause-and-effect conception of teaching and learning shaped most of the educational research programs for two decades following the Coleman study. Researchers viewed teaching as a discrete set of behaviors and tried to find whether different sets of behaviors were related to different learning gains by students. These researchers assumed a tight connection between teaching as a cause and learning as an effect that follows from the cause. The researchers were not burdened with fancy ideas about the nobility of teaching, nor did they pay much attention to the so-called inputs of education (such as the size of the school library, per-pupil expenditure, or the number of college recruiters who visited the school in a year). On the contrary, they went straight for the jugular. They had one burning question: Do the instructional behaviors of some teachers lead to systematic gains in student achievement, while different instructional behaviors by other teachers show no systematic gains in student learning?

It is because of the work of the behaviorists and other experimental psychologists that researchers possessed confidence in this way of phrasing the key questions. In addition, recent advances in research design and data analysis permitted researchers to look directly into classrooms for an answer. Moreover, the federal government, through the newly established National Institute of Education, was anxious to fund this research. If the researchers could show that what goes on in schools and classrooms does account for some of the variance in student achievement, the government's past investment in education would be vindicated and future investment would likely be continued.

At first the research programs yielded little in the way of tangible results. But gradually findings began to emerge showing that teachers do make a difference (one of the key books at the time was entitled *Teachers Make a Difference*[7]) and that what happens in schools does account for some of the variance in student achievement. To the best of our knowledge, no one has succeeded in showing that what teachers and schools do ever accounts for more than 15 percent, or at most 20 percent, of the variance in achievement. Still, that is no mean feat. Time in school does not consume more than 20 percent of the waking life of the student, so perhaps it would be unreasonable to expect that what happens there would account for any more of the variance.

The teaching behaviors found to be associated with optimum gains in student learning are those that we have already discussed as the executive approach to teaching. Now it should be clear why this approach is independent of content, context, and culture. The researchers set out to find the generic links between teaching and learning, using conceptions of teaching and learning gained from the work of behaviorial and experimental psychologists. They framed their studies to address the perplexing problems created by the Coleman Report and a government committed to achieving racial and economic equality through the provision of equality of educational opportunity. What they learned is that there are some instructional behaviors that are more frequently associated with high gains in student achievement than other instructional behaviors. These behaviors make up the executive approach to teaching.

Afterthoughts

This approach to teaching can be viewed as a very powerful one. No other set of instructional methods can lay claim to accounting for so much (relatively speaking) of the variance in student achievement. But consider this: Suppose we took teaching out of the typical school classroom and placed it in a tutorial setting. Suppose there are only two or three students to one teacher. And suppose further that these few students know why they are studying with this teacher and willingly choose to be part of an educational relationship. Do you think the executive approach to teaching would be of much value in this setting? It would seem that the knowledge and skill about engaged time, curriculum matched with evaluation, opportunity to learn, and all the other aspects of the executive approach are superfluous in this new setting.

Why? Because there is hardly anything that needs organizing or managing. The teacher is free to concentrate specifically on the students and on what they are learning. What does this perspective tell you about the executive approach? Take a moment to think about it. Let us see if your answer is the same as ours.

If the executive approach is unnecessary in a tutorial setting, yet seemingly necessary in a typical school classroom, then this approach to teaching may have much more to do with how we organize education in schools and how we engage learners in this form of education than it does with any root notion of what education is all about. To put it another way, the executive approach to teaching accounts for variance in achievement, not because it has been shown to be a particularly good way to educate human beings, but because it works well in rooms of 600 square feet that are filled with twenty-five young people, more than two-thirds of whom, if given a choice, are likely to choose to be somewhere else.

The executive approach to teaching seems to work because it fits so well the modern circumstances of teaching. If we changed the circumstances, the executive approach might be far less powerful. The power of the approach does not stem from any deep connection between it and any significant educational theory. Rather it is tied more to the structure of modern-day schooling: to classrooms with a lot of students; to accountability; to tests and report cards; to grade levels and diplomas; to teachers who are licensed to work with some children but not others, with some subjects but not others.

Still, these are the realities of the schools in which we work and learn. Are we compelled to adopt an approach to teaching that capitalizes nicely on the peripheral features of schooling, while leaving untouched many of the truly basic values that constitute our sense of what it means to be an educated person? Or are Fenstermacher and Soltis merely engaging in sophistry here, inasmuch as there is no inherent conflict in both managing a classroom as any good executive would manage a complex organization and, at the same time, pursuing and attaining the ideals of a fully educated human being? We hope you are stymied by this problem. It has been a difficult one for us to handle ourselves. The resolution might lie in looking at another approach to teaching. Before you begin the next chapter, however, we invite you to examine the relevant cases and disputes in chapter 6. If you take a few moments to work through those that bear on the executive approach, as indicated in table 1, you will not only have a better idea of this approach but also be better prepared to venture into an examination of the next approach to teaching.

Chapter 3

The Therapist Approach

Remember Mrs. Gardner, the art teacher? She started an art lesson on flowers by asking her students to think back to how they felt when they saw the colorful flowers on their way to school. What does how you feel about something have to do with teaching and learning? A great deal, especially in the therapist approach to teaching. But we have to be careful here. It is easy to trivialize this approach, reducing it to some formless amalgam of emotions, beliefs, attitudes, and opinions. Care is also required to avoid concluding that this approach has something to do with persons who are not mentally healthy. Though it might be a useful approach for those whose grasp of reality is less well developed, the therapist approach is intended to apply as much to the everyday activities of teaching as the executive and liberationist approaches. Just why this approach is called the therapist approach will become clear as the chapter unfolds. As we did with the executive approach, let us begin by considering what might be an actual situation.

You are hired to teach English to intermediate school children (say, grade 8). Some weeks before school begins, you start seriously preparing for the first weeks of school. What thoughts run through your head as you sit with paper, textbooks, and other class materials in front of you? Are you thinking about how you will approach the grammar lessons? The assigned textbook appears to do a good job of explaining key grammatical ideas, although you might want to expand some sections and shorten others.

How about literature? How will you balance linguistic and literary considerations over the course of the year? As you ponder these questions, you are probably thinking about the students—wondering about the best way to elicit their interest in what you plan to teach. But who are these students you have in mind? Do they have names? Do you know anything about them? What do they care about, and what is their interest, if any, in the study of English?

Individual Differences

Often when new teachers plan their instruction, they have in mind some prototypical student: someone like themselves, perhaps, or an archetype they recall from their own days as students. This conception of the prototypical student usually shapes the way a new teacher plans to teach the subject. Let us say this happens to you. You do all your preliminary planning with prototypical students in mind. It is not only convenient for you to do it this way, it may also be necessary; how can anybody really plan for students they have not seen? For that matter, how can anybody *really* take account of the lives of students? They differ in so many fundamental ways.

Just to show you how pertinent these doubts are, here is a sneak preview of your eighth-grade English class—the one you will not see for four more weeks. The characteristics or conditions of the learners are indicated, and the number of students who share each condition is shown.

Characteristic	Number of Students
English is not native language; speaks only native language	4
English is not native language; speaks English adequately	4
Physical handicap: missing thumb and two fingers on right hand	1
Moderate hearing impairment	2
Parents separated within the year	1
Parents divorced	6
First year in this school district; moved from more than a hundred miles away	5
Has extreme difficulty with spatial representation; possible neural damage	1
Detests English grammar	5
Loves English grammar	2
Shows no apparent feeling toward English grammar	13
Reads well above grade level	7
Reads at grade level	6
Reads well below grade level	11
Five merit badges short of Eagle scout	1
Physically abused by one or both parents	2
Traveled to more than five foreign countries	2

Traveled to more than five U.S. states	15
Never traveled beyond twenty-five miles of home	7
Has recurring nightmares; gets little sleep	1
Loves nearly all sports and rock stars	5
Is very selective about rock stars and sports	12
Enjoys building things	6
Responds well to freedom and responsibility	8
Responds well to structure and authority	8
Family survives primarily on welfare	3
Family consists of two adults and two children; no fewer than two cars and home larger than 10 rooms	3

If you just skimmed this list (a tendency many students have), maybe we should add one more characteristic to it. How about:

Rushes through detailed material, in hopes that author will summarize and explain point without requiring reader to ponder it	1

If you looked carefully at the characteristics of your future students, did you think of a way to deal with them pedagogically? Or did you find yourself wishing they would just go away?

You, as the teacher, have some choices here. You can ignore these conditions, trying to teach past them and hoping for the best. That may sound like a terrible thing to do, but a lot of teachers feel they must do so, at least part of the time. With twenty to thirty-five students in a class, a required amount of content to be covered, tests to be taken, and grades to be given, some teachers argue that they are simply unable to deal with the multiple characteristics of their students. Though these teachers have a point, there are alternatives to this position.

Another way to approach the individual differences among students is to acknowledge them, but more as impediments or facilitators to learning than as vital parts of the learning process itself. This point may seem like a distinction without a difference, but it is crucial to understanding the therapist approach to teaching. The teacher who treats student characteristics as impediments or facilitators to learning is placing a high value on the student's acquiring the content of instruction. There is a content, some x, out there, so to speak, that the teacher is trying to convey to the learner. The particular characteristics of the learner impede or expedite this process of imparting x to S, and the teacher tries to take these characteristics into account so that they support, rather than hinder, the acquisition of x. The individual differences of the student count only insofar as the teacher can use or surmount them to bring about the learning of some specified subject matter.

Features of This Approach

So far we have looked at two alternatives to dealing with student characteristics. You might ignore them, which, given the typical circumstances of today's classroom, is not always so heinous a deed as it may seem at first. Or you might acknowledge these characteristics in ways that diminish those likely to hinder learning and enhance those likely to facilitate learning. There is a third alternative. You might treat these characteristics as essential features of the learning process itself, as vital to everything the learner thinks, feels, and does. In this view, what the learner *is* cannot be separated from what is learned and how it is learned.

That handy little formula, $T\phi Sxy$, will help us amplify this point. In the executive approach, x symbolizes subject-matter content: geology, perhaps, or physics, history, or auto mechanics. The ϕ stands for the technical skills used to get x from its source to the learner, in a way that permits the learner to acquire x to some acceptable level of competence. The point of the activity (y) is the learner's acquisition of specialized knowledge. In the therapist approach to teaching, the character of ϕ is altered: Teaching is the activity of guiding and assisting the learner (S) to select and pursue x. The act of teaching (ϕ) is much less involved in preparing content (x) for S to acquire and is far more involved in preparing S for the tasks of choosing, working on, and evaluating what is learned.

The purpose of teaching in the therapist approach is to enable the learner to become an authentic human being, a person capable of accepting responsibility for what he or she is and is becoming, a person able to make choices that define one's character as one wishes it to be defined. To the teacher as therapist, the student's authenticity is not cultivated by acquiring remote knowledge that is unrelated to the quest for personal meaning and identity. Filling the student's head with specified knowledge that has been selected, packaged, and conveyed by others only keeps the student from grasping himself as a human being. It separates the student from himself by forcing him to attend, not to his own feelings, thoughts, and ideas, but to the sterile thoughts, images, and attitudes of others.

The teacher as therapist, dealing with the student characteristics described in the long list above, would neither ignore these characteristics nor try to use them as mechanisms to support the learning of some bookish content. The teacher as therapist would confront these characteristics directly, often openly with the affected student, and ask how the student plans to develop herself and experience her world, given her particular characteristics. The teacher as therapist does not accept responsibility for moving specific knowledge and skills from some outside source into the mind of the learner; rather the teacher accepts responsibility for helping the student make the choice to acquire knowledge of a given kind and for supporting the student as she acquires that knowledge and uses it to advance her sense of self.

How does one get an Educated-Person card according to the therapist approach to teaching? Answering this question requires breaking the rules a bit. The idea of such a card would be anathema to the teacher as therapist, for reasons that will become clear when we examine the existential foundation for the therapist approach. For now, we will bend the rules a bit. The card comes when the person is an authentic human being. To be authentic is to be geniune (not false or deceptive, especially to yourself), to take your freedom seriously, to understand that you have choices about who and what you are, and to accept the responsibility for making these choices and confronting their consequences.

The y in the therapist version of $T\phi Sxy$ is authenticity. That is the purpose of undertaking a relationship between teacher and learner. When that y is achieved, the E-P card is earned. In the executive approach, the y is specialized knowledge. Teacher and learner come together for the purpose of the learner's acquiring specific knowledge and skills. When the specialized knowledge and skills are mastered to some agreed level of competence (often determined by scores on tests), the E-P card is awarded to the learner. The x for the executive teacher is content selected by the teacher or curriculum specialist. In contrast, the therapist teacher is committed to assisting S to acquire the x of his choice. There is a definite difference. In the executive approach, $T\phi Sxy$ reads "the Teacher teaches (ϕ) x to S so that y (S acquires specialized knowledge)." In the therapist approach, $T\phi Sxy$ reads "the T guides and assists (ϕ) S in the selection and learning of x so that y (S becomes an authentic, self-actualized person)." Note that the object of the verb changes from the executive to the therapist approach; it is content in the former case, an attribute of the student himself in the latter case.

Given what you now know of the therapist approach, what is your reaction to it? Opposed? Favorable? Are you wondering whether you might be something of the executive, doing an effective job of getting students to learn school subjects, while also being part therapist, encouraging them to come to grips with what they are as human beings? Can you be both? Unfortunately, it does not appear that we are permitted to combine these two approaches, for they rest on very different conceptions of what it means to be a person. A brief look at the social and psychological foundations of the therapist approach will explain the logical proscription against using the two approaches together.

Roots in Social Criticism

In the previous chapter, we mentioned Lyndon Johnson's Great Society programs and the Coleman Report. Just before that era, education in the United States was making its closing adjustment to the great educational debate of the thirties and forties, traditional versus progressive education. As educational institutions sought an accommodation to progressive educational ideals, while remaining essentially traditional in structure and purpose, the Soviet Union launched Sputnik, President Kennedy was assassinated, President Johnson advocated both guns and butter (meaning the nation could both fight the war in Indochina and still support massive social justice programs), and our national awareness of the tight connections between schooling and equal opportunity for members of different racial and cultural groups increased dramatically. In the midst of this social and political unease, a number of educational theories were advanced.

The therapist approach was one of these theories. It arose from a fascinating conjunction of contemporary social criticism and a new version of psychology developed in opposition to behaviorism and experimental methods. Paul Goodman was one of the harshest and most read of the social critics. His *Growing Up Absurd* had the force of holy writ for the sixties counterculture.[1] Goodman's most pungent criticisms of education, however, are not in *Growing Up Absurd*, but in *Compulsory Mis-Education*[2] and in the many articles he wrote for magazines and journals. Writing for the *Saturday Review* in 1968, he strongly endorsed the view that we can "educate the young entirely in terms of their free choice, with no processing whatever. Nothing can be efficiently learned, or, indeed, learned at all . . . unless it meets need, desire, curiosity, or fantasy."[3]

In what seems like a direct swipe at the executive approach, Goodman argued, "It seems stupid to decide a priori what the young ought to know and then try to motivate them, instead of letting the initiative come from them and putting information and relevant equipment at their service."[4] The typical rejoinder to this contention was to point out that this way of educating the young may not be in best interests of the society in the long run. To which Goodman replied:

> If the young, as they mature, can follow their bent and choose their topics, times, and teachers, and if teachers teach what they themselves consider important—which is all they can skillfully teach anyway—the needs of society will be adequately met; there will be more lively, independent, and inventive people; and in the fairly short run there will be a more sensible and efficient society.[5]

At the time, this proposal was considered radical; it still is. Notice that Goodman gives a central role to choice for the learner. The learner chooses the content to be learned, when and how it is to be learned, and who is to teach it. The teacher's obligation in this setting is to enhance the learner's power to choose and to help the student use what is learned as an opportunity for personal growth. Herbert Kohl, another prominent advocate for alternative forms of education, comments on the teacher's role as an example in the life of the learner:

> Of course the teacher is a moral exemplar—an example of all the confusion, hypocrisy, and indecision, of all the mistakes, as well as the triumphs, of moral man. The children see all this, whatever they pretend to see. Therefore, to be more than an example, to be an educator—someone capable of helping lead the child through the labyrinth of life—the teacher must be honest to the children about his mistakes and weaknesses; he must be able to say that he is wrong or sorry. . . . It is the teacher's struggle to be moral that excites his pupils; it is honesty, not rightness, that moves children.[6]

Humanistic Psychology

Many of the educational ideas coming from these social critics were rooted in an alternative psychology known as humanistic or "third-force" psychology. Gordon Allport, Abraham Maslow, and Carl Rogers were among the leading figures in this school of psychology. Each of these psychologists stresses the uniqueness of individuals, and the difficulties that psychology, in its attempts to become a science of mind or behavior, has had in treating the individual with proper regard for his or her unique properties.

Maslow does not deny the behaviorist contention that individuals act in response to stimuli, but he argues that this action must be understood as the result of an interaction between the person's needs and the unique "lifespace" of every person. Each one of us has a hierarchy of drives from basic survival needs for food and water to such higher-level needs as to give and receive love, to develop self-esteem, and to appreciate beauty. A person who interprets his situation effectively and thereby meets his needs to the highest level possible for his lifespace is, according to Maslow, a self-actualized person. A fully self-actualized person is one who possesses a balanced and integrated personality, with such positive traits as autonomy, creativeness, independence, altruism, and a healthy goal-directedness.[7]

The goals of self-actualization and authenticity are quite compatible with one another. The teacher as therapist seeks both, insofar as he or she strives to develop students with healthy personalities, able to plan, choose, and act in ways that advance their own growth and development. Although many educators have embraced Maslow's notion of self-actualization, Maslow did not develop its implications for education. It is to the work of Carl Rogers that we must turn for the pedagogical implications of humanistic psychology.

"Teaching," claims Rogers, "is a vastly over-rated function."[8] "It is most unfortunate that educators and the public think about, and focus on, *teaching*. It leads them into a host of questions which are either irrelevant or absurd so far as real education is concerned."[9] He bases this view of teaching on the importance of what he calls "experiential learning." This is learning that is filled with personal involvement; the whole person is *in* the learning event, not a passive absorber of whatever the teacher dispenses. It is learning that is self-initiated. It is pervasive; it influences every aspect of the learner's being. It is evaluated by the learner, not by the teacher or by tests. It is rooted in meaning, which is to say that the learning has personal meaning for the learner; it advances the learner's power to understand and influence events that are important in his or her life.

Learning of this kind cannot be controlled by a teacher. It must be determined by the learner. The teacher can only guide, suggest, perhaps encourage, maybe even, when the occasion is appropriate, warn. Rogers believes that "anything that can be taught to another is relatively inconsequential and has little or no significant influence on behavior."[10] What is important is not what can be taught, but rather what is learned. "The only learning which significantly influences behavior is self-discovered, self-appropriated learning." This self-discovered learning constitutes truth that is "personally appropriated and assimilated in experience."[11] Because learning of this type is *personally* appropriated, it "cannot be directly communicated to another."[12] Thus the teacher is not one who imparts knowledge and skill to another, but one who helps another gain his own knowledge and skill. In the role of guide or facilitator, the teacher must be "a real person in his relationship with his students. He can be enthusiastic, he can be bored, he can be interested in students, he can be angry, he can be sensitive and sympathetic. Because he accepts these feelings as his own he has no need to impose them on his students."[13]

Humanistic psychology, as Maslow and Rogers make quite evident, is a psychology based on freedom, choice, personal growth, and the development of emotional and mental health. In their view, education makes a significant contribution to these ends, but not by the traditional mechanisms of packaging subject-matter content for delivery to student learners. Instead, the student must be helped to attain his or her own realization. The teacher's task is to direct the learner inward, toward the self, so that the learner is thereby enabled to reach outward, choosing the content to be acquired and the actions that follow from mastery of this content.

What is your view on being an executive and a therapist? Can you do both? Not if you accept Rogers's argument. He contends that you cannot put knowledge in someone's head (not in any way that is meaningful), as the executive approach would have you do. Any attempt at teaching in the executive manner will diminish the learner, keeping him from appropriating and assimilating that knowledge in his own experience and thus keeping him from realizing the meaning and the freedom that leads to living an authentic and self-actualized life. To the humanistic psychologist, the executive approach leads to alienation by driving a wedge between the knower and the known. When the teacher becomes the executive, the learner always acquires someone else's knowledge, on someone else's terms, for someone else's purposes. There seems no compromise possible here, no way to have the cake of the therapist and eat it as an executive.

Is there really no way to bridge the gap? It seems not. Recall that the executive approach is grounded in a behavioristic, experimental psychology, which itself is grounded in the philosophy of logical empiricism or positivism. Positivism is a philosophical position regarding knowledge that elevates to the highest levels of regard observation in the natural world, public testability of hypotheses, objectivity, and verifiability of claims. It was most fully developed in the late nineteenth century. In a somewhat modified, contemporary version, positivism provides the sustaining concepts for our modern view of science. The languages of purpose and freedom, of feelings and emotions, and of subjective and spiritual experience that are important to the humanistic psychologist are generally *verboten* in the positivist-behaviorist world.

Existentialism

In contrast to positivism, the undergirding philosophy for humanistic psychology is existentialism. In the minds of many, positivism and existentialism are archenemies. It would take us far afield to explore existentialism in any depth, but we can touch on just enough to complete the description of the therapist approach to teaching. One of the few tenets that existentialists hold in common is that existence precedes essence; that we simply are before we are anything in particular. One of the best known existentialists, Jean-Paul Sartre, explains:

> What do we mean by saying that existence precedes essence? We mean that man first of all exists, encounters himself, surges up in the world— and defines himself afterwards. If man as the existentialist sees him is not definable, it is because to begin with he is nothing. He will not be anything until later, and then he will be what he makes of himself. . . . Man is nothing else but that which he makes of himself. That is the first principle of existentialism.[14]

We become something as we confront the world and choose our way through it. If we avoid these choices and their consequences, then we are, in fact, avoiding what is the essence of being human: our freedom. It was Sartre who wrote of persons fleeing from their freedom. They did so because absolute, total freedom is so frightening. It is hard to confront the view that we may do differently anything we are now doing; that we can always choose to act another way, think a different thought, feel a new emotion. Yet to be authentic, we must confront our freedom, we must create meaning for ourselves, and we must choose our way to and through our future.

Do you recall Mr. Provider from chapter 1? He is the math teacher who wants his students to learn the formula for computing the area of plane surfaces bounded by straight lines. Note that he has in mind some x, formulas for computing area, that he wants to get across to his S's. He is a mathematics teacher, and thus mathematics is what is covered in his class. Most students are in this class because they are assigned to it. Mr. Provider would, of course, be delighted if his students took a sustaining interest in mathematics, and he will try many tricks and ploys to gain their interest. But in the end, say the humanistic psychologist and existentialist, it will come to nothing. The students did not choose to learn about computing area. There is little in their lives that would lead them to personally appropriate and assimilate this knowledge. Mr. Provider is not charged with the responsibility for, nor is he really interested in, enhancing the capacities of his students to choose, to gain in personal identity, and to enlarge their sense of power and meaning.

What do you think of Mr. Provider? Is he damaging the minds and stunting the psyches of his students? Or is he legitimately pursuing an alternative approach to teaching? Whatever you might think at this moment, is it clear why there is a problem with trying to be both executive and therapist, at least at the same time? Perhaps you are considering being an executive on some occasions and a therapist on others. To which the existentialist might scream, "You either believe that students should be presented with the content to be learned, or that they can and should determine their own learning. You either believe that a teacher can teach some specific content to a learner, or that the teacher can only guide the learner in the pursuit of specific content. You believe that the purpose of education is either to instruct the learner in knowledge and skill, or to engender authenticity and self-actualization. CHOOSE! You cannot sit on the fence. You cannot do both."

Afterthoughts

If you are befuddled by this problem, pulled in two directions, you are not alone. The split between the positivist-behavioristic and the existentialist-humanistic approaches is one of the classic antagonisms in modern philosophy and psychology. Walter Kaufmann states the disjunction well:

> It is one of the saddest features of our age that we are faced with an entirely unnecessary dichotomy: on the one hand there are those whose devotion to intellectual cleanliness and rigor is exemplary but who refuse to deal with anything but small, and often downright trivial, questions; in the other camp are men like Toynbee and some of the existentialists who deal with the big and interesting questions, but in such a manner that the positivists point to them as living proofs that any effort of this kind is doomed to failure. Aware of their opponents' errors, both sides go to ever greater extremes; the split widens; and the intelligent layman who is left in the middle will soon lose sight of both.[15]

Kaufmann says the dichotomy is entirely unnecessary. It is not clear to us what he means by that contention. There are two distinctively different views of humankind here. On what grounds could one say that it is unnecessary for these two views to clash with one another? Perhaps he believes that if the two camps would simply agree to meet together, then . . . what? What about you as a teacher? Can you effect a resolution of your own, something that will enable you to use both approaches in the classroom? We have not left you with much hope for doing so, have we?

While you ponder these questions, there is a small detail that we would like to clean up. While discussing the therapist's approach to the Educated-Person card, we stated that advocates of this approach to teaching would strongly oppose any such card. Why? Because each person is unique. As each person chooses his or her way into a self-projected future, that uniqueness is maintained. Thus there is no shared standard or common outcome that can be used to determine when someone qualifies for the E-P card. There is no specialized knowledge here that is certifiable by a College Board test or a Graduate Record Examination. You could, perhaps, choose to award an E-P card to yourself, but why would you want such a thing? It would not mean anything to anyone else, inasmuch as you awarded it to yourself on the basis of your own uniqueness.

And herein lies a difficult problem for the therapist approach to teaching. Each person is unique. This uniqueness is maintained by making choices. You must make the choices on the basis of the future you construct for yourself. But what of the future of others? What of the future of the community? The state? The nation? May not these entities exercise jurisdiction over schooling in order to insure some common meaning and serve common purposes? Should not the government of the people impose a shared program of studies on each child in order to preserve the culture and the nation?

In the United States it has long been accepted that the maintenance of democracy and national identity requires a common education. This is generally made manifest as a common core of studies for all students. Once this core is acquired, then students may usually select from a range of programs and courses or, if old enough, leave school altogether. But first, the common good must be considered. How, then, are we to tolerate the students' choosing the time, place, and content of their education, as the therapist approach would have it?

Again, your desire, like ours, may be to look for compromise. The therapist approach is so attractive, so filled with dignity and hope for each human being, that we resist letting go of it. But, as we have asked before, how can you have both and be at all consistent with the principles and imperatives of either approach? Everything about each approach says, "Choose!" What will you do?

Before trying to decide the issue, we would like you to consider the cases and disputes that table 1 links to the therapist approach. You will find these in chapter 6. Then we will examine one more approach. It is not a compromise approach, nor is it some sort of resolution of the paradox that behaviorism and humanism pose. This third approach places great emphasis on the x in $T\phi Sxy$ and comes out looking quite different from either of the approaches considered thus far.

Chapter 4

The Liberationist Approach

The two approaches examined thus far stress different variables in the $T\phi Sxy$ formula. The executive approach highlights what the teacher does (ϕ). The therapist approach emphasizes what the student (S) is and chooses to become. The approaches each have different purposes (which appear to be mutually exclusive, given the arguments just sketched). The executive teacher strives for the learner's acquisition of specified knowledge and skill. The therapist teacher supports and guides the learner in becoming an authentic person. We have considered every variable in the formula save one. Though x has been mentioned often, it has not been featured until now. The liberationist approach to teaching brings content, x, to the forefront.

A Case Study

To illustrate the liberationist approach, we would again like you to imagine yourself a teacher. This time you have just completed college with a double major in math and physics. You are very proud of that achievement. And even prouder that you turned down several job offers with private industry because you want to be a teacher. You have long regretted what you regard as the poor preparation secondary students receive in math and the natural sciences. You love these fields and look forward to sharing your knowledge with your students. You have your pick of schools; preparation like yours is not an everyday occurrence for beginning teachers. You select a fine high school in a middle-class, racially mixed suburban community.

You have five periods, two of physics and three of math. One physics class is advanced placement (AP), the other is general physics for students contemplating college. One math course is pre-algebra, the other two are algebra I classes. You prepare extensively for these courses, supplementing the textbooks with workbooks, your own custom-made supporting materials, and a full range of visual aids, including colorful charts and graphs, posters, slides, filmstrips, even a few movies depicting famous scientists and mathematicians struggling with the great intellectual problems of their times.

In each course, your interest is that as many students as possible will confront the material in the way a physicist or mathematician might. For example, you decide to begin the unit on electricity simply, by using a flashlight or ordinary house lamp as a starting point. But before the first period of that lesson is over, you plan to consider circuits, polarity, resistance, and current flow. From there you will introduce the basic mathematics typically used in electrical computations, and then the atomic character of electrical and electronic circuits. Along the way, you will introduce the students to Gilbert, Faraday, Maxwell, and Neumann. By the end of the unit, you hope to have covered conduction, resonance, filtration, and magnetic effects, as well as thermal and biochemical effects.

How do you plan to teach all this content? That troubles you a bit, but not excessively. You know the material well. You feel certain you can bring it alive for the students through careful use of instructional aids, through historical and biographical sketches, and by involving the students in exercises and experiments that bring them face-to-face with problems to be solved. You are concerned about how to communicate this complex material to classes containing a range of different students—different abilities, different experiences, different interests—although here again you are not overly troubled. You are confident of the value of your material for the students and are prepared to make adjustments as you learn about their differences.

Features of This Approach

This heavy emphasis on content, with much less emphasis on specific teaching skills or the psychic and emotional states of your students, makes you a candidate for the liberationist approach. But only a candidate. Full membership requires consideration of the purpose of teaching beyond the emphasis on content, just as consideration of purpose is essential to the therapist and executive approaches. Mere emphasis on the student does not make you a therapist: you must focus on the student for the purpose of helping him become authentic. Mere emphasis on the technical skills of teaching does not make you an executive; you must also seek the student's effective acquisition of specific knowledge and skill. Mere emphasis on content does not make you a liberationist; you must aim at freeing the student's mind from the limits of everyday experience, from the deadness and banality of convention and stereotype. Thus the content of your physics and math classes must be selected and organized for the particular purpose of liberating the mind of the student.

You might object at this point, saying that so far you cannot tell the difference between *x* in the executive approach and *x* in the liberationist approach. Both deal with knowledge, and both appear to deal with specific knowledge, although the liberationist approach appears to describe that knowledge at a high level of sophistication. But surely mere differences in depth and scope of knowledge cannot be the only things separating the executive *x* from the liberationist *x*. If that is your retort, take a bow. You are right on target.

The nature of the knowledge and the way it is explored are different in the executive and liberationist approaches. The *x* in the executive approach is, as we pointed out earlier, highly specified. It is made up of discrete facts, ideas, topics, and domains, often expressed in the form of behavioral outcomes or measurable competencies. This kind of tight specification is required if objective, standardized tests are to be used to determine what, if anything, the learners gained from their teachers. Recall that the teacher's task is to move *x* from its source to the mind of the learner. The manner of this instruction seems quite determined by those technical skills of teaching that have been proven effective for producing gains in specified knowledge.

In the liberationist approach, the manner of instruction is heavily influenced by the content itself. For example, as a science teacher, you hope your students will become critical, skeptical inquirers, because that is a prerequisite mindset for doing good science. In order for the students to learn to think in this way, they must see it being done (it is unlikely that it will be learned from reading the text). *You* are the teacher who must serve as the model for the students. If you wish them to become critical inquirers, as the nature of your subject demands, they must observe you doing critical inquiry. To model it, you often have to *do* science in your classroom, so that they can see what it means for them to do science as critical inquirers. It is nonsense for you to expect them to behave critically and questioningly about phenomena in the world when the person who teaches the subject does not act that way.

Manner in Teaching

This way of acting as a teacher is called "manner." Not the "manner" of "table manners" (though akin to it), but the "manner" of "I like his manner." A manner is a relatively stable disposition to act in a given way under circumstances that call for such action. We speak of persons who are gentle, humorous, affectionate, secretive, ambitious. These words describe their manner. Under appropriate circumstances, an affectionate person will smile, touch, hug, offer support, and ask sympathetic questions, while the same circumstances might lead a person of shy manner to become quiet, frown, and pull away.

The manner of the teacher is critical to the liberationist approach, for it determines, in large measure, whether the knowledge and skill to be learned will free the mind or simply trap it with dull and irrelevant facts and skills. One of the foremost contemporary advocates for the liberationist approach, R. S. Peters, illuminates the idea of manner as he discusses what he calls "principles of procedure" for teaching such subjects as science or history:

> There must be respect for evidence and a ban on "cooking" or distorting it; there must be a willingness to admit that one is mistaken; there must be non-interference with people who wish to put forward objections; there must be a respect for people as a source of argument and an absence of personal invective and contempt for what they say because of who they are. To learn science is not just to learn facts and to understand theories; it is also to learn to participate in a public form of life governed by such principles of procedure. Insofar, therefore, as a person is educated scientifically, he will have to absorb these principles of procedure by means of which the content of scientific thought has been accumulated and is criticized and developed.[1]

These principles of procedure are part of what we mean by manner. Note that Peters speaks of showing respect for evidence and for people as a source of argument; of not interfering during the presentation of alternatives; of not using invective and showing contempt for different views. These are manners (consistent ways of behaving) that the teacher must display in order to teach science well. The teacher must not only display these manners, but call attention to and encourage their imitation by students and give praise when students exhibit these manners themselves. It is not enough for the liberationist that knowledge and skill are simply acquired, no matter how fully or completely. They must be acquired in a manner appropriate to the kind of knowledge it is.

In the teaching of literature, for instance, the manner of instruction might be somewhat different from that of science. Here the teacher might wish to exhibit and encourage passion and involvement, while the teaching of science calls for dispassion and detachment. In art and music, the teacher might show disregard for the conventional rules of harmony, balance, rhythm, or color in order to encourage creative expression in the medium, whereas it is only under very special conditions that the scientist may disregard the methodological rules of conventional scientific inquiry. Each major subject field typically has a set of manners, principles of procedures as Peters call them, appropriate to that field.

If we have described the idea of manner with sufficient clarity, we can add a little complexity to this discussion without throwing you off stride. Not only is the manner of teaching influenced by the *nature* of the content (for example, physics, literature, or art), it is also influenced by the *sophistication* of the content. If the content is undeveloped and low level, what value and fascination could possibly accompany such content? Unsophisticated content gives the teacher little range and depth of manner. This situation might be compared to an actress faced with a poor script. She does not want to play it because it will not challenge her thespian talent; it denies her range and depth.

The specified knowledge so valued in the executive approach is especially subject to this shortcoming. The knowledge and skills are so highly specified in order that the learner's accumulated fund of knowledge and skill can be diagnosed accurately, an instructional prescription prepared, instruction given, and, finally, an unambiguous evaluation administered. The difficulty is that knowledge and skill are specified at so basic and detailed a level that it becomes impossible for the teacher to impart it in a manner that reflects anything but a rudimentary, sometimes even primitive, approach to the content. This outcome is much less likely in the liberationist approach because there is a strong emphasis on sophisticated content.

Moral and Intellectual Virtues

We will look more carefully at this notion of sophistication in a moment. Right now there is one detail about manner that needs to be added. We discussed manner that is specific to subject fields and how this manner is affected by the sophistication with which the content is developed for the classroom. There is also what might be called general manner. Its form and character are not dependent on the different fields; it is applicable across all fields. This general manner is usually grouped under the heading of "moral and intellectual virtues." Among the moral virtues are honesty, integrity, fair mindedness, and just treatment. Among the intellectual virtues are reasonableness, openmindedness, regard for evidence, curiosity, a reflective habit of mind, and judicious skepticism.

Each of these denotes a manner of behaving that the liberationist would insist be characteristic of all teaching. Indeed, these moral and intellectual virtues are considered part of the content of the liberationist approach. They are to be acquired by the learner just as the knowledge and skill in the subject field are to be acquired. Whoops! Did you catch that? We have been rolling along here speaking of manner and content as if they were two different entities, and now we just said that manner is part of the content. Take a moment. See if you can sort this out on your own. Then come back to the text.

Manner is part of the content of instruction because all the time you are imparting the content of some subject to the students, you are also imparting the way you approach and deal with that content. Students learn not only from what you say and assign to them, they learn from the way you do it. Typically you might not think much about this facet of teaching (it is part of what is meant by the notion of "hidden curriculum"), but to the liberationist it is a vital part of instruction. The liberationist wants the student to acquire the manner (general and special) as well as the content, for the content without the manner will not be liberating.

Traits of Character

It may be hard to see how manner becomes part of content, because it cannot be taught to students directly, as can knowledge, skills, and understanding. These latter outcomes are achieved through a kind of frontal attack. But there is another type of learning outcome, called "traits of character." It differs from the other three because it is difficult to approach directly. It sounds a bit silly for a teacher to say, "Today I am going to teach you kindness," although it does not sound silly to say, "Today I am going to teach you the Pythagorean theorem," or "I am going to teach you how an atomic reaction is initiated and sustained." Traits of character are taught through example and model, not by direct instruction. As such, they must be part of the manner of the teacher if they are to be acquired by the learner. However, even though they are taught indirectly, they are still very much a part of what the liberationist teacher wants the student to learn. This feature is what makes manner part of content. The British philosopher Gilbert Ryle, looking at such traits as hard work and fair mindedness, offers a helpful description:

> What will help to make us self-controlled, fair-minded or hard-working are good examples set by others, and then ourselves practising and failing, and practising again, and failing again, but not quite so soon and so on. In matters of morals, as in the skills and arts, we learn first by being shown by others, then by being trained by others, naturally with some worded homily, praise and rebuke, and lastly by being trained by ourselves.[2]

Ryle contends that we learn traits of character by being shown and trained, with encouragement or reprimand, as appropriate. We master the trait by finally training ourselves to live it well. This is the way the student aquires manner from the teacher. The well-known child psychologist Urie Bronfenbrenner makes a similar point:

> However important genetic factors may be in the determination of human behavior, it is quite clear that such qualities as mutual trust, kindness, cooperation, and social responsibility cannot be insured through selective breeding; they are learned from other human beings who in some measure exhibit these qualities, value them, and strive to develop them in their children. It is a matter of social rather than biological inheritance. Or, as one of the author's teachers, Walter Fenno Dearborn, used to put it: "He's a chip off the old block—not because he was knocked off it, but because he knocked around with it."[3]

There is little that is more destructive of the liberationist approach than calling for a manner from students that is neither possessed nor exemplified by the teacher. Each of us has had teachers of this kind: the science teacher who asks for critical thinking from students, but never veers from the problem sets in the text or the answers in the teacher's edition; the art teacher who talks incessantly about being creative and expressive, but always structures the assignment and has rigorous standards for neatness in the art room; the elementary school teacher who admonishes students to share, but yells when anyone forgets a pencil or touches any of his materials on the back table.

The liberationist teacher is careful to serve as a model for the special and general manner required to free the mind of the learner from dogma, convention, and stereotype. If creativity is required, this teacher does not teach a unit on creativity; creativity is not so much a skill to be taught directly as it is a way to approach tasks and activities. So the teacher acts creatively, calling on students to follow the lead and offering the opportunity and safety for them to try being creative. The same is true for critical thinking, for compassion, and for fair play. These and many other key traits are acquired indirectly from instruction that also aims at imparting knowledge, skill, and understanding.

Forms of Knowledge

A while ago we distinguished the nature of the content studied from the level of sophistication at which the content is developed and presented to students. We promised to return to this point after discussing manner. It is time to do so. Remember that content in the executive approach is highly specified, as it must be if the teacher as executive is to function well. These demands on content stem primarily from past experience with what kind of content children are most likely to master, plus the requirement that this content be developed so that it can be assessed accurately at a later time. The demands of the liberationist approach are quite different. A teacher inclined toward the liberationist approach believes that the mind can only be developed and freed by the acquisition of a broad range of fundamental knowledge and understanding, combined with the most fitting intellectual and moral traits of character. What is included in the category of "fundamental knowledge and understanding" must not be determined simply by what children are most likely to learn successfully or by what can be tested with the greatest reliability and validity.

The liberationist places some strict controls on what counts as knowledge and understanding, and thus on what is proper to the curriculum. One of the most thorough contemporary explications of these controls has been put forward by P. H. Hirst.[4] He argues that knowledge can be divided into seven forms. They are mathematics, physical sciences, human sciences, history, religion, literature and fine arts, and philosophy. Hirst states that these seven forms or domains cover all the kinds of things we as human beings can come to know about in the world. The best education is the one that initiates students into these forms of knowledge.

In addition to a concern for *what* the proper forms of knowledge are, the liberationist also places stipulations on *how* the forms should be taught. That is, you can neither pick just any topic for instruction (you must, if your goal is to free the mind, select from among the forms) nor approach it any way you please. For Hirst, a form of knowledge has some special characteristics that can help the liberationist teacher see what is fundamental and what is mind building about a subject. A form of knowledge is a coherent conceptual system that humankind has collectively developed over time to make sense of particular areas of human experience. Each form has its own special concepts that capture key aspects of human experience.

For example, to make sense of artistic experiences, we need a concept of beauty; to make sense of experiences in the natural, physical world, we need such concepts as truth, fact, and evidence; and to understand mathematical phenomena, we need the concept of number. Besides these key concepts, each form of knowledge, according to Hirst, has a distinctive logical structure of its own (think of the different geometries of Euclid, Riemann, and Lobachevsky), a set of special skills and methods for making knowledge claims in that form (think of scientific method), and a set of unique standards for publicly testing and judging claims (think of literary or artistic criticism).

These notions may seem excessively complex. One reason some of us have difficulty grasping them is that we have not, ourselves, had many teachers who fully understood and were committed to the liberationist approach. Thus we find it hard to assimilate liberationist notions into our own experiences with education. For this reason, it might be helpful to simplify some of the ideas just covered. We will try not to do violence to these concepts by transforming them into somewhat more ordinary ideas and metaphors, but it would be a good idea if you reread the material of the last few pages after you finish the next few paragraphs.

As we grow and develop, we experience the world around us. Information and data come into our heads through our senses. We listen, see, feel, hear, and taste things in the world. We can do several things with what enters our heads. We can, in a manner of speaking, toss it right back out (forget it or ignore it). We can store it for a short period of time and not give much thought to it. We can ponder it, wonder about it, and even do something about it. We can elaborate on it, connect it with some other things, and perhaps create new information or ideas. Of course, everything that happens inside our heads has an influence on the information that we continue to gain through our senses. What we know and feel about our world can have a profound impact on what we will look and listen for, what we will see, and how we will interpret what we see, feel, and hear.

Let us call all this entering information and data "input." How we filter, process, and structure this input is a critical matter to the liberationist. The forms of knowledge mentioned above are considered to be among the very finest means for imparting structure to experience—for giving experience profound and useful meaning and for empowering us to control and mediate our experience. These forms of knowledge are not comprised simply of facts, figures, and formulae; they are key or central ideas, distinctive logical structures, methods of inquiry, and publicly held standards of judgment. If we learn these latter characteristics of the forms while we learn the facts, figures, and formulae, then we have truly made knowledge the basis for freeing the mind from the limits, deceptions, and conventionality of ordinary, unstructured experience.

A teacher might consider himself a liberationist if he stresses content, the x in $T\phi Sxy$. However, if the content is seen merely as facts, figures, and formulae, the teacher is not a liberationist, even though x seems to be the emphasized variable in that person's instruction. Remember that in addition to imparting subject-area content, the liberationist teacher must also exemplify the manner of a liberally educated person; he or she must possess and model the moral and intellectual virtues we discussed earlier. Now there is another wrinkle: The content itself must be developed in particular ways. It must be planned and presented so that the learner can grasp the root structure of the various forms of knowledge, and in this way the learner is enabled to structure his or her own experience.

The structure of the content is, according to Hirst and many other educational theorists, revealed by attending to the key concepts of a given form, its distinctive logical structures (the rules and heuristics that govern the way concepts and knowledge claims connect), its methods for undertaking formal inquiry (such as scientific method, historiography, ethnography, or phenomenology), and its standards for testing and judging hypotheses or claims. Thus, to acquire a discipline (physics, chemistry, history, psychology, and so forth) is to learn its major ideas, understand its logical structure, be able to undertake controlled inquiry within its domain of experience, and know what determines the merit and worth of your findings or productions.

The notion that knowledge has a form or structure has long been a part of liberationist thinking. It received a great deal of attention in the curriculum development movement of the 1960s, spurred on by the now-classic book by Jerome S. Bruner, *The Process of Education*. Bruner wrote that "grasping the structure of a subject is understanding it in a way that permits many other things to be related to it meaningfully. To learn structure, in short, is to learn how things are related."[5] Bruner then discussed the importance of key ideas:

> The basic ideas that lie at the heart of all science and mathematics and the basic themes that give form to life and literature are as simple as they are powerful. To be in command of these basic ideas, to use them effectively, requires a continual deepening of one's understanding of them that comes from learning to use them in progressively more complex forms.[6]

It is not surprising that we would draw on Bruner to help us describe the nature of content in the liberationist approach. He is a cognitive psychologist and, as such, represents a different school of thought from the behaviorism of the executive approach and the humanistic psychology of the therapist approach. Because the cognitive psychologist is especially interested in the way we acquire, interpret, apply, and expand our knowledge, there is a close affiliation between the liberationist and the cognitive psychologist. However, it would be an error to press this point too far, for the liberationist approach is not nearly so rooted in psychology (of any kind) as the executive and therapist approaches. The parentage of the liberationist approach is more philosophical. To the extent that this approach would call upon psychology for assistance, however, cognitive psychology would be the preferred school of thought.

Bruner's ideas about the structure of knowledge and how it is acquired led to many curriculum reform projects, including some that may have been a part of your own school studies. The new math of the 1960s was one of these efforts, along with such projects as the Biological Sciences Curriculum Study (BSCS), the Science Curriculum Improvement Study (SCIS), and the highly controversial Man, A Course of Study (MACOS). It is not likely that you encountered the last curriculum. Bruner had a significant part in its development, but it irritated some powerful political constituencies, leading the U.S. Congress to withhold federal funds from agencies that supported the development and dissemination of MACOS. Many of these so-called new curricula have not survived the accountability and back-to-basics movements of the late 1970s and the early 1980s. One idea that retains its appeal for teachers inclined to the liberationist approach, however, is Bruner's claim that "the foundations of any subject may be taught to anybody at any stage in some form."[7]

The Paideia Proposal

We have already noted that the liberationist approach is rooted much more deeply in philosophy than psychology. These roots may be traced back to Plato and Aristotle. In a sense, the notion of liberal education is decidedly Greek. Philosophers still turn to the works of Greeks (and such Romans as Horace, Virgil, and Cicero) for the basic premises of liberal education. The Greek idea of *paideia* is at the conceptual core of the liberationist approach to teaching.

Paideia is the name of a system of education offered in classical Greece and Rome. Its curriculum included gymnastics, rhetoric, philosophy, natural history, music, grammar, mathematics, and geography (note the parallels to Hirst's forms of knowledge). These are the subjects we often think of today when we think of liberal education. Their study makes a person "well rounded," prepares the person generally for life. During the early Christian era, the Greek notion of *paideia* was thought of as *humanitas*—the culture of humankind. In both *paideia* and *humanitas* the focus is on the capacity of human beings to achieve the most noble ends, the highest attainments in knowledge, understanding, and virtue. These notions of excellence in human attainment have persisted in Western thought. They were fundamental notions during the Renaissance and the Enlightenment and continue to be so into the present day. In one form or another, philosophers throughout history have argued for the liberationist approach: not just Plato and Aristotle, but also Erasmus and More, Pascal and Descartes, Hume and Voltaire, Mill and Kant, Whitehead and Dewey.

Just a few years ago a number of books and reports on the state of education in the United States were released. Perhaps the most well known is *A Nation at Risk*, issued by a national commission. Another report receiving widespread attention is entitled *The Paideia Proposal*, by Mortimer J. Adler. Decrying the practice of tracking high school students into different preparatory curricula, Adler says:

> Of all the creatures on earth, human beings are the least specialized in anatomical equipment and in instinctive modes of behavior. They are, in consequence, more flexible than other creatures in their ability to adjust to the widest variety of environments and to rapidly changing external circumstances. They are adjustable to every clime and condition on earth and perpetually adjustable to the shock of change.
>
> That is why general, nonspecialized schooling has the quality that most befits human nature. That is why, in terms of practicality and utility, it is better than any other kind of schooling.[8]

Specified knowledge, the goal of the executive approach, is anathema to Adler. Using school time to prepare persons for specific tasks, skills, or jobs is a misuse of school time. The most practical learning is general learning, learning that equips us to realize our adaptability and enables us to perform such tasks as we may confront in a rapidly changing world. General, or liberal, learning is best not only because it capitalizes best on human adaptability and intelligence, but also "because it prepares our children to be good citizens and to lead good human lives."[9]

How would Adler achieve these ends in school settings? His modern answer is not markedly different from the ancient answer. The course of study set forth in *The Paideia Proposal* is a case in point. Adler argues for three major goals: (1) the acquisition of organized knowledge, (2) the development of intellectual skills, which include the skills of learning, and (3) enlarged understanding of ideas and values. Under the first goal, Adler includes three primary areas of subject matter: language, literature, and fine arts; mathematics and natural science; and history, geography, and social studies. Does this sound familiar? We hope so, for these are the forms of knowledge that Hirst contends are critical to the liberationist approach. Adler's second and third goals should also be familiar to you, for you have previously encountered them as part of the discussion of manner in the liberationist approach.

Afterthoughts

The strong emphasis on subject-matter knowledge has troubled many who have looked closely at the liberationist approach. They ask whether it is truly possible or even desirable for all students to study the basic subjects in the way the liberationist argues, especially given the broad range of individual differences in most classrooms. Can all students develop the academic and scholarly minds espoused by the liberationists, or is this approach to teaching really an elitist view of education because its goals can be attained only by a select few? What would be wrong with a more practical approach, aimed at developing the skills and understanding needed for everyday life and work? Indeed, some critics have said that the real question is not the range of differences among students but the range of differences among teachers, that many teachers are simply not able to master and teach the liberationist approach well. Do you agree?

Others argue that the liberationists present too coherent and uniform a picture of knowledge. They contend that most scholars cannot agree on the structure of knowledge in their fields, or if, in fact, there really is any such thing as *the* structure or even *a* structure of knowledge. Even were some agreement on structure possible, the key concepts and logical forms change over time, making it unwise to try to teach these notions as if they were inherent features of the discipline. The liberationist retort, of course, is that this criticism is essentially defeatist and leaves the teacher with no guidance whatsoever.

Jane Roland Martin, an American philosopher of education, argues that the Hirst-Peters conception of the educated person as someone who has a fully developed mind and has attained a broad cognitive perspective is simply too ivory-tower and narrow a view of what it means to be an educated person. She says:

> The great irony of Hirst's theory of liberal education is that it is neither tolerant nor generous; it conceives of liberal education as the development of mind, restricts the development of mind to the acquisition of knowledge and understanding, and restricts knowledge to true propositions. . . . The received theory's liberally educated person will be taught to see the world through the lenses of the seven forms of knowledge, if

seven there be, but not to act in the world. Nor will that person be encouraged to acquire feelings and emotions. The theory's liberally educated person will be provided with knowledge about others, but will not be taught to care about their welfare, let alone to act kindly toward them. That person will be given some understanding of society, but will not be taught to feel its injustices or even to be concerned over its fate.[10]

Did you get the sense as you read this chapter that the liberationist approach was so heartless as Martin implies? If she is correct, might there be a way of linking the therapist and liberationist approaches, so that the x and the S in $T\phi Sxy$ could both receive emphasis? Or is there a logical and conceptual chasm separating the therapist and the liberationist approaches, just like the one that separates the therapist from the executive? It is time to grapple with these thorny questions, and we will do so in the next chapter. Before you turn to it, you will gain a sharper sense of the liberationist approach by working through the "Freedom and Indoctrination" dispute in chapter 6. You may also want to look at some of the other cases and disputes recommended for this chapter in table 1.

Chapter 5

Reflections on
the Three Approaches

Are you ready to decide, or have you already made a decision? Are you confused? Inasmuch as the three approaches appear so different from, even inconsistent with, one another, we tried to pose them in a way that calls for a choice on your part. Let us say you are ready to consider adopting one of the three positions. On what grounds might you choose? There are two simple questions you ought to ponder before deciding: What are the proper standards for an Educated-Person card? What should schools do to qualify persons for this card? Two simple questions? Perhaps not, but trying to answer them may help you considerably in clarifying your choice.

Education and Schooling

For example, let us say that you believe the proper standards for an E-P card are competence in such basic skills as reading, writing, and computation, plus a good liberal education (that is, $y =$ specified knowledge + a liberated mind). Both of these educational purposes are important to you. But you further believe that the school should be held responsible only for the specified knowledge part of this goal—that is all that can be tested for anyway. Thus even though you believe a person is not fully educated until he or she achieves a liberated mind, you also believe that the school can only be responsible for part of this achievement—the part that involves preparation in the basic skills. Liberation of the mind, you contend, is a lifelong process achieved by participation in the larger social setting, the world beyond the school.

If this were your position, you might select the executive approach. It promises to prepare students in the basics in the most effective and efficient manner. The selection seems justified according to your view of the school's proper role in education. And the distinction you make between education and schooling is a good one. Perhaps we should not automatically assume that schools are responsible for everything that makes up a good education. Contributions to education are also made by other institutions like museums, libraries, churches, and performing arts centers, and by parents, peers, the media, and the community. Schooling is just one of the contributors to the E-P card.

Some persons take exception to this view, arguing that education must be a very special activity. It is not something acquired here and there, made up of a little of this experience and a little of that experience, some from school, some from home, some from television, and some from life itself. Their view of education is that it should be undertaken to *structure* the experiences we have, not simply be another experience. The philosopher Harry Broudy puts the point rather bluntly:

> When life predicaments can be resolved with common-sense generalizations, one learns by living; when common sense is insufficient, one has to learn by comprehending knowledge discovered and formulated by others. How far do common sense and personal experience go, these days, in thinking about pollution, inflation, the problems of health and peace?[1]

Do you recognize the liberationist approach in these words? Broudy probably would not claim that everything needed for a *first-rate* E-P card should be found in schools, but he would argue that what is found in schools must be quite special—not just another set of ordinary experiences, but the development of disciplined knowledge and understanding that enable students continually to enlarge their horizons, come to grips with the problems and possibilities of life on this planet, and gain a sense of place in the past, present, and future of the human race. It has already been argued (in the last chapter) that the attainment of such laudable goals requires the teacher to explore sophisticated conceptions of knowledge in the traditional subjects and to give careful consideration to the development of manner.

You were cautioned that there are problems with this view. When these noble goals are applied in a system of mass, compulsory schooling, they can have effects just the opposite of the intended goals. Instead of promoting a just, compassionate society, the liberationist approach can and often does end up a great advantage to the highly intelligent and the well-to-do, and a dead-end street for the poor, the racial or ethnic minority, or the less intellectually able from any population of students. The price, it seems, of emphasizing content in the form of highly elaborate conceptions of knowledge is that the teacher leaves behind the very students that many think ought to be ones school really helps (the wealthy and intellectually able will take care of themselves, or so the argument goes).

So far, the choices do not seem terribly attractive. On the one hand we can teach as executives, limiting the content to basic knowledge and skills, while ignoring the lifespace of the learner in our effort to move x efficiently and effectively from source to recipient. Or we can seek to liberate the mind of the learner by exploring knowledge and developing manner in great depth, only to find that the major benefactors of this approach are those who are already economically and academically advantaged. What about the therapist approach; does it represent a way out of the dilemma?

Social and Political Realities

It seems not. Here we must depend on the student to select the content and accept the guidance of the teacher in how to meet and master this content. As a social and political matter, no modern society seems willing to offer choices of this kind to all its students. In these societies, social and political needs usually take precedence over the needs of the individual. For too many key persons—parents, taxpayers, and politicians—the therapist approach appears to be a kind of anarchy. For these persons, school is a place where children must not only learn the basic knowledge and skills needed to function in society, they must learn the game of life—that we cannot do anything we choose to do, that fate and foolishness deal us gentle strokes and hard knocks, and that the world is not peaches and cream.

The obvious personal appeal of the humanistic and existentialist positions does not negate the influence of social and political demands on schools. The existentialist may be correct in asserting that we are free and that the only authentic life we can lead is the one we constantly choose our way toward. It may indeed be true that we are unique and that there are no models to which we must conform, no templates into which we must be squeezed. And it may be that anything worthwhile can only be learned by oneself, never taught by another. Despite these eloquent sentiments on behalf of the individual, we are, as a practical matter, unable to teach in this way in schools as they are. Furthermore, there are sufficient problems of theory and concept with the therapist position to make us wonder whether we should teach that way even if we were permitted to do so.

That last comment may not be fair. As the disputes in chapter 6 show, there are problems of theory and concept with all three approaches, not just the therapist approach. These problems have been compounded by the preceding discussion, where the practical matter of what schools are has been introduced into our deliberations about the three choices. Until this chapter, we have suggested that the choice is yours, to make on such grounds of reason and ethics as you are able to muster. Ahhh, were life so simple! There are practical matters as well. What does society seek from its schools? What demands will the parents of your students make on you? Do they not have a prior right to determine the kind of education their children will receive? And then there are some crass, but vital, considerations: How will you be evaluated by the principal and judged by your colleagues? What will determine the increments in your salary? How does one advance up the career ladder in schools?

How Shall I Teach?

Now what? Does the position you formulate take account of these real-world exigencies and thus become something of an amalgamation of theory and reality? Or should you ignore these practical matters for now, formulate your position intellectually, then modify it as you gain experience? Or should you just throw in the towel and let life move you along, as the ocean current moves the kelp? These are tough dilemmas, for they raise one of the root questions every human being must confront: How shall I live? Except now the question is a subset of that one: How shall I teach?

We began this chapter by stating that the selection of an approach to teaching would be aided by answering two questions: What are the proper standards for an E-P card? What should the schools do to qualify students for this card? The implication here is that you can answer these questions on your own, without further consideration of the social, economic, and political realities of the context in which you will teach. That implication has now been shown to be incorrect. Any answer that is likely to serve you well must take account of these realities. But there is a critical difference between *taking account of* the realities and allowing them to *determine* what and how you teach.

If you begin with some clear conception of what education is, as a human endeavor of body, mind, and spirit, you have the opportunity to control many of the practical forces that impinge on you, rather than falling victim to these forces. If you have some sense of the place and purpose of schooling in the education of the young, a sense developed from reflection on theory and ideal, you can shape and direct these realities in ways that support your aspirations for your learners. This activity is not always a struggle of your ideals against the powerful negative forces of the world, for there is much in schools that is already founded on good theory and high ideals. Yet you are not likely to recognize what is there, in either good form or bad, if you cannot recognize where you yourself are.

Thus the first task every teacher must face is to come to some conclusions about the nature and purpose of being an educated person and the place of schooling in achieving this status. These conclusions should be firmly held views, but never set so deeply that they cannot be modified or even uprooted by new experience and insights. The three approaches to teaching we have explored with you here are offered in this spirit: to enable you to begin forming your concept of education and the place of the school within it. We set the approaches up as if they were mutually exclusive, but we did this only as a way to clarify their differences and to illustrate the power and appeal of each of them.

Irreconcilable Differences or Integration?

These are, after all, only *approaches*: different ways of thinking about the same thing, teaching. They provide ways of separating out a myriad of conflicting conceptions so that we can see more clearly what similarities, differences, and problems there are within the jumbled confusion of contemporary educational theory and practice. They do rest on theoretical and ethical ideas that seem logically opposed to one another. Yet we believe that the logical boundaries that separate these positions as scholarly constructions, as ways of thinking about teaching and education, need not be barriers to practical action.

You can, for example, be an executive at times, a therapist at others, a liberationist at still others. In fact, there seem to be situations in teaching that call on you to do just that. There is the fourth-grade student who can barely read or write. You may wonder how he got this far, but he is yours to teach as best you can. Perhaps the best way to help him is to exercise the technical skills of the executive teacher as proficiently as you can. And what of the battered child, who stares through you and barely speaks? Before you can move much of any kind of x to that child, you must help her deal with a world that has overwhelmed her. The learners who are fully up to speed may profit from the liberationist approach, exploring knowledge and manner as deeply as their abilities permit.

Did that last sentence disturb you? It was a "ringer." If you use the liberationist approach only for learners already "fully up to speed," you may exacerbate the conditions of inequality in schools. Then only the more able learners would receive the advanced content and instruction, and that would place the less able learners at an increasing disadvantage. There is a clear danger to education if these approaches are integrated in certain ways. If you think of these approaches as options to be selected for different learners or situations, you run the risk of condemning students to preestablished categories for instruction. This sometimes happens in the case of ability groups and in the tracking that occurs in secondary schools. When grouped in these ways, learners can become trapped in their assigned categories. The incorrigible learners are taught by therapists and allowed to self-select what they will learn (not because we believe that is the right and proper way to educate, but because we have no luck getting them to do anything else); the average learners are instructed by teacher-executives so that they acquire the so-called basic competencies; and the advanced learners are encouraged to delve deeply into the broad range of human knowledge. And thus the gap among the incorrigible, the average, and the academically able grows greater and greater.

From a practical standpoint, some of this differentiation is an inevitable consequence of good instruction, no matter what approach is used. That is, those who are ready and able to gain from school will do so more quickly and more completely than those who are less ready. The absolutely critical consideration is to avoid predetermining who will gain, and at what rates, by teaching one group of children according to an approach that keeps them from growing in ways that another group is growing from their exposure to a different approach. Maxine Greene, a philosopher of education who has struggled with these same problems, argues that whatever the teacher decides,

> he will not *impose* values or virtues on students; he will *pose* questions, do what he can to move them toward increasing awareness, deepening conviction. Granting them dignity, freedom, and autonomy (unless they are little children), he becomes a catalyst in the process of their self-identification, their learning how to learn. . . . No matter who he is, he will not deliberately guide his students toward a boring, empty, dissatisfying life; he will not deliberately encourage the development of dispositions he believes to be destructive or "bad."[2]

Endthoughts

You have probably guessed where we are leading you. The normative nature of teaching demands a commitment to worthy educational values, and each of these three approaches contains something of value. If you are committed to having your students gain to the fullest extent possible from their experiences of schooling, we believe you must try to put these three approaches together somehow while avoiding the pitfalls of doing so. We also believe that this task is not so impossible in practice as the theoretical differences in each approach suggest. It is not easy either.

Integration will require a sensitivity to factors in concrete situations that call for a delicate balancing of your values, purposes, and actions. There are no easy recipes and you may not always succeed. Of course, you may decide, for good reasons, that the advantages of adopting one approach far exceed the disadvantages of attempting integration. Your choice of a normative view of teaching should rest on your own best judgment. This is why we have offered a consideration of the negative as well as the positive features of each approach in this book. The choice is yours. In the end, if our position is tempting, you will have to decide whether integration is worth trying. We can only offer some observations that have helped us in our own teaching to try to honor these different points of view.

The executive approach demands technical skill as a teacher. This skill need not be employed solely to move some highly specified x from source to recipient, though it often gets articulated that way because highly structured curriculum materials and standardized testing requirements so frequently accompany calls for the executive approach. However, we believe you can learn useful techniques, develop effective pedagogical skills, and hold yourself accountable for proficient instructional capabilities without forfeiting the opportunity to explore content areas in depth, as the liberationist would. And you may even view the development of manner as part and parcel of these instructional skills.

Thus it seems possible that the teacher as executive, who in practice attends to content and manner as a liberationist, would be far ahead of a teacher who is only an executive or only a liberationist. Such a teacher would be aware of how to manage a classroom, how to structure learning activities, how to organize student time and tasks, so that he or she could quickly come to grips with the sophisticated content and accompanying manner of the liberationist approach to teaching.

But if you were to adopt the technical skills of the teacher as executive to support the attainment of liberationist goals, would you have to ignore the life history and personal autonomy of the learner? Could you be an executive, a liberationist, and a therapist at the same time? As we have frequently pointed out, you cannot be all three in theory and still be logically consistent and conceptually coherent. As a practitioner, however, we believe you can understand and adapt the scholar's distinctions and dilemmas in ways that enable you to do what the theorist cannot do:

Be a sensitive, rational, flexible human being in concrete educational situations while trying to balance worthy multiple goals.

How can you achieve the final integration of the therapist point of view into your teaching? By not attending exclusively to content as it appears in books and tapes and films, but by also attending to it as it appears to the minds and hearts of the learners. Your aim should not be simply to get the learners to acquire the knowledge, skills, manner, and understandings that you teach, but to enable and to empower them to grasp, interpret, use, and extend what is learned in ways that advance their own identity and meaningfulness. The wisdom of humankind must be appropriated by the learners, made their own, and worked out for themselves.

So, in the end, if you would try to integrate your approach to teaching you must seek to free not just the mind but the heart and the spirit as well. To do this, you must compromise the theoretical purity of the three approaches and dig deeply into what humankind knows and understands and into yourself to learn what the known means to you and how you will live. And you must do this for your learners, before your learners, where they can see the manner of an educated person and choose to model themselves after you. Then you truly will have become a teacher.

Chapter 6

Cases and Disputes

To this point we have examined three approaches to teaching and have asked you to think about them along the way. They each have much to commend them, and yet each has potential negative features. To help you reflect on and develop your own examined approach to teaching, this last chapter contains a series of realistic vignettes—in the form of cases, dialogues, and disputes—that raise a number of issues, including ethical issues not dealt with extensively or directly in the text. As you read them and discuss them with others, you will have an opportunity to articulate and examine some of your most heartfelt beliefs about teaching. They will also give you the opportunity to bring theory and practice closer together by showing you that how one thinks about and approaches one's teaching makes a real difference in how one acts and reacts as a teacher in real-life situations.

To give you an overview of the topics we have treated in these selections and the major points at issue in them, we have provided a summary (see table 1) from which you can select cases and disputes of special interest to you. Of course, we could not treat all possible topics and issues, nor could we anticipate those that would be of major concern to you when you are using this text. So you should feel free to write

TABLE 1. Summary of Cases and Disputes

Page	Title*	Issue
60	Grading Policies (1)	Do different approaches call for different kinds of student evaluation?
62	An Educated Person (1)	What is essential to becoming truly educated?
63	School and Approach Mismatch (1)	Should a teacher change his or her approach to be more in line with school policies?

*A number in parentheses after a title indicates that the case or dispute is recommended for use with that specific chapter.

TABLE 1. (*Continued*)

Page	Title*	Issue
64	Teacher—Engineer or Artist? (2)	Is teaching an art or a science?
66	Individualized Learning (2)	Does research provide infallible materials and techniques?
67	How Much Control Is Too Much? (2)	What are the advantages and disadvantages of the executive approach?
68	Workbook Dilemma (2)	Should the teacher or the administrator be the executive?
69	A New Science Kit (2)	Do curriculum materials reflect a technological mindset and limit teacher creativity?
70	Individual and Societal Needs (3)	Can the school serve both individual and social needs without conflict?
71	Curing Shyness (3)	Who determines the direction of personal growth, teacher or student?
72	What Standard Shall We Use? (3)	Should a teacher grade on personal growth and individual progress?
73	Teaching "Relevant" Literature (3)	What happens if students object to a teacher's approach?
74	Teacher and Mother? (3)	What happens if a teacher's personality and an approach do not fit?
75	Freedom and Indoctrination (4)	Can the mind ever really become free through education?
76	Too Young to Be Critical? (4)	Is developing a critical mind age related?
77	Education for Life (4)	Is a liberal education for everyone?
79	Freedom of Speech? (4)	How open minded must a teacher using the liberationist approach be?
80	Mass or Class Culture? (4)	Is the liberationist approach elitist?
81	Learning Chemistry by Discussion (5)	Is the liberationist's manner efficient?
83	Different Learning Styles (5)	What factors decide choice of approach?
84	Compatibility of Approaches (5)	Must a teacher choose an approach?

your own cases and disputes or to bring issues from your own experiences into your class discussions.

Some of you may have already sampled these cases and disputes when following the suggestions we made at the end of each chapter. To indicate our recommendations of issues related to specific chapters, we have placed a chapter number in parentheses following the title of each case or dispute. Of course, you should feel free to use them in any order suitable to your interests and purposes. Many of the cases and disputes in this chapter also reach beyond the neat conceptual lines drawn around the three approaches described earlier in the text, demonstrating that the real world of education is not as neatly packaged as textbooks and scholars sometimes make it out to be. This is not to say that thinking initially about teaching in terms of the heuristic scheme of the three approaches dealt with in this book is useless. Rather, it is to warn that when theory and reality meet, you need to accommodate your categories and schemas to the world in which you live and work, making reasonable adjustments that will allow you to pursue your most basic beliefs and values. We also hope you will see that which name you give to your own approach to teaching is not as important as what you really believe about the purposes of teaching and what it means to be an educated person. Therefore, we hope you will use these cases and disputes as a bridge to the real world so that you may become a thinking and responsible teacher no matter what your approach.

Grading Policies

David Levine is the chairperson of Henry Hudson High School's Social Studies Department. Because of the size of the student population, several sections of certain courses are offered each year, and each is taught by a different instructor. In the case of Modern American History, three teachers offer courses. Students are assigned to these courses according to a simple alphabetical rotation. But this simple system has created a complex problem for Mr. Levine, for each teacher uses a different approach and parents and students are complaining that this is unfair.

The first section is taught by Albert Foley. Mr. Foley is a young, somewhat idealistic teacher who believes that stimulating learning experiences form the core of an education. In his class, he relies upon the study of current events from newspapers and television, and he encourages his students to initiate independent study projects. Mr. Foley is not as concerned about command of exact facts as he is about the personal significance that modern American history may come to hold for his students. In that direction, he believes, lies the promise of good citizenship and authentic personhood. Students are graded on the basis of essays they write about topics they select and journals of personal response to classroom discussion and current events. He grades because he has to, but he does not believe grading is what education is really about. Among the students, he is known as "Easy A Foley." In a typical year, 40 percent of his students will receive A's and another 30 percent will receive B's. The rest are given C's, with an occasional D for serious cases. Mr. Foley says that a student will pass his class if he is able to find his way to the classroom. In his opinion, it is hard enough being a teenager, and he is not going to make it any tougher. He believes that his students really learn and grow in their sense of self-worth because of his teaching and grading policies.

"Historical knowledge broadens and deepens the mind" might be the motto of Mr. William Sampson, the teacher of the second section, for he believes that subject matter is all-important in getting students to understand the world they have inherited. Mr. Sampson relies on the textbook exclusively, and he delivers detailed lectures. He demands that his students know the facts about American government and recent historical events, and he has little patience with uninformed opinion. He wants his students to use evidence from historical events and documents to back up their claims. In his view, good citizenship must rest on a sound foundation of knowledge and the ability to think critically. He tells his students that they must learn American history backwards and forwards or they will not pass his course. But his exams are not on the specific facts of history. Rather, he gives rigorous and demanding essay exams that force his students to think about history. In a recent class of forty students, Mr. Sampson's grades were distributed in the following manner: three A's, five B's, eighteen C's, nine D's, and five F's. Mr. Sampson contends that his tests are fair measures of his students' ability to think. The students call him "Slasher Sampson."

Nancy Wright, the teacher of the third section, has taught history for twelve years, and each year she tries out new ideas and techniques she has read about in *Social Studies*, a national journal for teachers. This year she has developed a behavioral-objectives unit on the New Deal and has designed an evaluation instrument for it that gives her very accurate ways for grading a student's knowledge of FDR's policies. She has found that specifying her own objectives not only helps her but also helps her students see clearly what they need to study and learn in her classes. Each year she feels that her teaching is still improving. One thing she does not change, however, is her policy of grading according to a curve.

In her most recent group of forty students there were five *A*'s, ten *B*'s, fifteen *C*'s, seven *D*'s and three *F*'s, a distribution of grades which she came to favor long ago after taking a course on statistics and evaluation. Ms. Wright uses both essays and objective tests in order to provide an unbiased basis for her judgments. She believes that her proportional approach to grading avoids the possibility of favoritism and accurately reflects the performance of each student as it compares to that of others in the class. Ms. Wright's students have no nickname for her.

Consider these different approaches to teaching and grading. Do you favor one over another? Why? Does each approach necessitate the kind of evaluation procedure used by each teacher, or could each use one another's grading policy without altering their approach very much? Does an approach also dictate the content in a course? Is this situation as it now exists fair to the students? What would you do if you were Mr. Levine?

An Educated Person

A: I was in my philosophy class today, and it really started me thinking about what it means to be a truly educated person.

B: It's really quite simple, isn't it? All that's required for becoming an educated person is graduation from a high school or a college.

A: It doesn't matter which? It doesn't matter what track or program or major you take?

B: No, it doesn't matter. Education is education, and each individual should have the kind of education he or she is best suited for. As long as a person learns what he or she is required to learn in order to graduate from whatever school, then in my book they're entitled to be called an educated person.

A: OK. Let's not argue about how much education you need or whether high school or college is sufficient. I don't think it's how long you go to school that counts anyway, as much as what you learn. But according to you, it doesn't even matter *what* you study or learn as long as you graduate from somewhere. Well, suppose there was a school where only math was taught. Would a person who only learned math and didn't know much about other things like history or science or art really be an educated person?

B: I see what you mean. That might be too narrow an education. I just mean that to really be educated, people should study what they are best suited for. They should be allowed to develop their own unique potential and identity. That's what being properly educated is all about; of course, you have to study other things so your education won't be too narrow. All schools and colleges require that, don't they?

A: That's just the point. It's the "other things" that make you a truly *educated* person. What you learn for yourself helps you become the unique *person* you will be, but what you learn in common with others is what makes you *educated*. So the problem is what "other things" does everyone need to study to become educated persons.

B: Math, history, literature, science, art—you know—the basic subjects.

A: And if you really learn them, then you're educated?

B: Of course.

A: Even if you never learned to care about other people or to be honest or fair? Is learning subjects all that education is about or is being educated and becoming an educated person more than that?

B: What more is there?

What do you think? To what degree is becoming educated developing one's unique potential and to what degree is it learning common things so that we can share and participate in our common cultural heritage as equals? Is there more to it than either of these two things?

School and Approach Mismatch

Janet had taught history for several years at a junior college. Tired of lecturing and longing for a change, she decided to try working at a different level in the education system. The public schools were not hiring, so she accepted a job with a small, conservative, church-affiliated secondary school at a considerable reduction in salary, even though she was neither conservative nor religious. She agreed to teach four sections of freshman history and one of remedial junior English, with a total of 143 students.

Janet found teaching high school challenging and exciting. She liked being with the students and even relished lunchroom duty, because it afforded her the opportunity to observe student interaction and to interact herself. Accustomed to dealing with adults and high school graduates, she treated her students with respect and genuine care. In a short time she developed an easy relationship with her classes and became known as an adult who could be approached. Janet made a habit of coming to work early every day in order to be available for those students who wanted to shoot the breeze or needed to talk seriously.

There was usually someone waiting for her, occasionally a student other than one of her own or even a fellow teacher.

As much as she loved and was rewarded by her work, she found dealing with the school's administration to be very difficult. Janet's personal philosophy of education emphasized discovery, opening the world for the student. She attempted to create a proper relaxed atmosphere for this. The school's position stressed adherence to rules, deference to authority, and strict norms of acceptable behavior. There was a rigid curriculum that was to be dispensed by the teacher and learned by the students. Teachers were responsible for seeing to it that all students learned this material. A proper distance between teacher and students was always to be maintained.

Janet soon found herself in conflict with the administration over these policies. Each classroom had a two-way speaker, and it was known that the principal and the attendance secretary occasionally listened in on class sessions. During the third week of school, Janet had been called on the carpet for allowing excessive noise in her classroom. When she apologized to her neighbors, she discovered that the complaint had not come from them but from the attendance secretary, who had been eavesdropping on the public-address system. Her colleagues also told her that the principal was dissatisfied because she was not covering the prescribed curriculum. Janet was furious about the way her teaching had been "observed."

Janet obviously faced a year at school in which she would often be acting in ways directly opposed to administrative goals and philosophy. But she needed her job.

In light of that economic reality, ought Janet to change her approach to teaching to be more in line with the administration's? Might it be possible to find a compromise approach? Should a teacher compromise his or her approach when it does not match the school's philosophy? What about professional autonomy and integrity? Do you think the "observation system" in this school is proper? What would you do if you were Janet?

Teacher—Engineer or Artist?

A: The practical importance of science is clear. It provides us with knowledge we can use in curing diseases, in exploring space, and in helping students learn. Education, no less than medicine or space exploration, must rest on a solid foundation of knowledge about how to do it.

B: I don't deny that knowledge about teaching like time on-task or how to design valid multiple-choice questions can be useful to a teacher. But when you come right down to it, teaching is an art. You can know your subject matter and materials, have a good grasp of learning theory and methods, and know the latest research findings, but when you're there in the classroom, your performance has to be more like an artist's than like a mechanical engineer's. Each teacher is a unique person, and it is by being yourself that you really become a good teacher.

A: A good teacher is an effective teacher, a teacher whose students learn! That can only happen if you think about your goals, carefully plan your lessons, select the appropriate techniques you will use, and exercise good judgment as you're teaching. If that is like being an *engineer*, so be it. It's not your artistic uniqueness that's important, it's your knowledge, experience, and executive ability that counts.

B: But what about those unanticipated teachable moments, those unplanned things the teacher as artist does that really get students excited about learning? What makes teaching come alive is the artistic talent of the really good teacher, not what he or she knows about the "science of teaching."

C: You both make good points. I'm not sure you really can separate the artistic from the scientific in any serious human endeavor. The good surgeon is as much artist as scientist and so is the good teacher.

A: If, by calling a surgeon an artist, you mean that he effectively executes his skills, I would agree. But that just makes my point. Both the surgeon and teacher depend on the knowledge gained through research that proves one technique or method better than another, more effective in curing patients or in getting students to learn. It is the scientific knowledge that makes it possible to get the best results.

B: But don't you see what you're both assuming, that a better teacher is simply one who *produces* more learning regardless of subject matter and regardless of effects on students. That's a one-sided, mechanical view of teaching. An artistic view seeks to make the educational experience of students more self-fulfilling, more personally relevant, and more satisfying, and only a sensitive artist can do that.

A: Would you rather be evaluated as a teacher on an agreed-upon set of competencies you are expected to demonstrate by means of an instrument developed and validated for the purpose—or by some "art critic" supervisor who may or may not like your brand of art?

How would you prefer to be evaluated as a teacher? As an artist? As an engineer? Do you think that someone who takes the executive approach to teaching is less inclined to see things other than learning goals as important in teaching? What might such other things be?

Individualized Learning

Bob was a first-year teacher in a fifth-grade open classroom. Bob, like all the other teachers of his teaching team, had responsibility for one homogeneously grouped math class. The math program of the school was designed according to the latest research in the following manner: Each student progressed through a series of worksheets; when one worksheet was finished correctly, the student went to the next. In this way, skill in addition, subtraction, multiplication, and other areas was to be learned at an individual's own pace. The idea was that the teacher could give individual attention to those children who needed it. Research had shown that at this grade level individualization was most effective.

Bob thought this system made sense. The students seemed to like the class, too. They were rewarded by the evidence of their progress and by the praise Bob gave when papers were completed.

Before long, though, Bob began to be uneasy about the direction his math class was taking. He felt that he was not really "teaching" his students. They were just doing worksheets on their own. He had thought he would be able to work one-on-one with the children. Instead, he found he spent almost no time with anyone. There was constantly a line of five or six children either waiting to ask questions or waiting to have papers checked. Bob felt that he could not afford to give as much time to each child as he would have liked, since it would be unfair to keep all the others waiting. The children who finished papers were congratulated and sent on to the next worksheet. The students who had questions were told to try to work out an answer by themselves. They often would, but this usually took the form of three or four unsuccessful guesses before the correct answer was stumbled upon. Furthermore, Bob was so busy at his desk that he had difficulty being sure students were working and behaving as they should. Some students seemed to be progressing much too slowly. Bob was concerned that this was because he had not watched these pupils closely enough. In short, Bob came to see himself less as a teacher and more as a "paper pusher."

Bob's worst fears seemed to be realized one day when he held an addition game. Bob chose problems that all the students should have known, since they came from worksheets all the students had completed. Contrary to Bob's expectations, many of his students were unable to do the problems he chose. It appeared that, indeed, many of Bob's students were not learning.

If you were Bob, what would you do? Do you think that Bob, knowingly or not, was using a teacher-as-executive approach here? Did his approach cause the problem and/or did it help him diagnose the problem? Why do you think research showed one thing about individualization and Bob found another? Was Bob really teaching?

How Much Control Is Too Much?

Elsie Simmons, a new teacher, was having second thoughts about the way she was teaching her junior literature class. At the start of the school year, her principal and colleagues had told her that the students she was getting were a rambunctious group—bright and eager, but in need of firm control. This, plus the fact that Elsie was a beginning teacher, had prompted the advice that Elsie exercise decisive control over the group from day one. Otherwise, they would take advantage of Elsie's inexperience. Research has shown that this technique produces the desired results.

Elsie took their suggestion to heart. She prepared meticulous lesson plans so that the class periods would always be under her control. And she stuck to these. The students were given specific readings to do and lists of questions to answer. During class, Elsie saw to it that she was always in charge, either through lecturing or directing questions to students.

As she looked back on things, Elsie saw that her teaching had been successful in one respect—the students were not behavior problems. The trouble was that they were too passive. They did not seem to "get into" the material. Elsie saw none of the enthusiasm and creative energy that this group was noted for and that they demonstrated in their other classes. At best, the class's work was adequate. In addition, Elsie was upset that many of the students seemed to resent her.

Elsie had hoped to make the literature course one where students could exchange ideas and express themselves. It did not seem to be working that way. Though she knew she would like to alter things, Elsie was not sure how or whether this could be done at this point. What should she do?

How might this teacher modify her approach? What are the pluses and minuses of an executive approach? Is this approach inappropriate for Elsie, or is it the way Elsie had implemented it that is at fault? Was this form of the executive approach a necessary first tactic?

Workbook Dilemma

Julie Karajian is a kindergarten teacher. She is considered one of the best teachers at P.S. 21, and in fact has been the subject of a documentary for network television and several articles on teacher excellence in various publications. Her philosophy of teaching is that children learn from experimentation and exploration. From this approach, Julie believes, children derive knowledge from relevant experiences and also develop an essential self-confidence needed to master future skills. Julie adapts each year's curriculum according to the type of class that enters in September. Activities reflect the group's unique learning styles. Julie is not a firm believer in the use of workbooks and learning kits, unless they are directly relevant to the children's abilities and backgrounds, which Julie has found they usually are not.

Mr. Jackson is the principal of P.S. 21. He is more interested in controlling the students in his school than anything else. He does not see children as unique individuals with specific styles of learning. Rather, he believes that most children fit into two categories: bright and not bright. He thinks teachers need to mold the children to a particular methodology, rather than vice-versa. He is aware of the diverse cultures from which his students come, but he believes that in order to survive in the real world children in this school must learn to get along as adaptive adults. He is also confident that workbooks and learning kits serve two significant functions in his school: to control students by keeping them busy and to serve as guidelines for what gets taught.

Recently, however, he has been approached by Julie concerning her class's new workbooks. She believes that because of their age level, developmental level, and cultural backgrounds, these children will find the workbooks stifling and irrelevant. Instead of using them for a total of two hours a week as required, Julie proposes not to use them at all. Mr. Jackson recognizes Julie as the best in the school, but he firmly believes these children need to become familiar with workbook usage and that use of the workbooks will teach them skills necessary for success in first grade. At the same time, he knows that children who come out of Julie's class often do the best in the first grade, so maybe they do not need the books as much. Besides, he has heard that Julie is tired of battling the administration and is thinking of moving to a private school. If she does, P.S. 21 will lose its greatest asset. But if the other kindergarten teachers find out that she is not using her workbooks, they will undoubtedly be angered that they are required to do so. Furthermore, what if Julie's children do not learn the necessary skills because they are unfamiliar with workbooks?

What should Mr. Jackson do? Is there some sort of compromise that could be reached? What should Julie do, as the teacher who knows her children best and who is confident about her approach to teaching? Should the teacher or the administrator be the executive?

A New Science Kit

It was the first teacher preparation day of the new school year, and Emma Dill was in her fifth-grade classroom unpacking the new materials that had arrived for her during the summer. After finding places for the paper clips, thumb tacks, and new construction paper, Emma turned to the gem of her shipment, a new science kit.

The district curriculum director, in consultation with a committee of principals and teachers, had decided on the new science curriculum to replace the textbook series that previously had been used throughout the district. Emma had served on the committee and had enthusiastically supported the choice.

Emma was one of those teachers who enjoyed teaching science. She never considered it a "filler" to finish out the last twenty or so minutes of the day. She always allotted plenty of time for science. She scheduled as many experiments as possible.

The main selling point of the new kit was that it involved experiments almost exclusively. Furthermore, all the materials except for a few common consumables were included in the kit, no small consideration in light of the time and energy Emma had spent collecting the things needed for experiments suggested by the old science text or developed by Emma herself. Even further, Emma had noted to herself with a certain amount of glee, all those teachers who had refused to do the experiments Emma considered so vital to the study of science would no longer have a way to avoid doing them.

Unfortunately (fortunately?), however, Emma had taken a summer workshop on school and society and had learned of neo-Marxist criticisms of schools. Neo-Marxists argued that the schools reproduced working-class mindsets in the children, and at the time she wondered if that really could be true. As she looked through the science kit now, she felt her enthusiasm for it wane. The kit consisted of several units. Each unit was comprised of a series of activity cards stating the purpose, materials, procedure, and questions for each activity. There were five copies of each activity card, so that several small groups of students could all work at once, moving in order through each step. There was a basic serial organization of the activities and units, and it was essential to do all activities in one unit before moving to the next. Students were to be rewarded in terms of the number of units completed. Emma reflected that these features, which last spring had appeared to her to offer opportunities for experimentation, pupil involvement, and pupil self-direction, now appeared different. She wondered whether the sources of the virtue of the kits—organization and self-sufficiency—represented hidden liabilities. The kit stressed pupils' following directions over personal interaction with the teacher, prescribed goals over goals developed by the teacher and the class, following a recipe over developing a method, and so on. In short, Emma was troubled by the thought that rather than giving her students an exciting encounter with science, she was really instilling technobureaucratic values, just as the neo-Marxist theorists warned.

Do you think Emma has accurately assessed the situation? Are her fears justified? Should she use the kit? Do curriculum materials based on an executive approach to teaching reflect a technological mindset and limit teacher creativity?

Individual and Societal Needs

A: Think about it; each of us has only one life to live. Education should help each person make his life meaningful and fulfilling as an individual. You can't do that by forcing students to learn what they don't find personally meaningful just because it happens to be in the curriculum guide.

B: What would you teach them then?

A: It's not *what* you teach that's really important. Don't you see? It is helping children and adolescents become themselves. Too many students just pass through the system and get treated in a mechanical way as we sort and train them for meaningless jobs and empty lives in our materialistic society. We should help them become their own unique selves.

B: That sounds good, but did you ever try to run an office or a factory full of "own unique selves"? There's nothing wrong with being yourself on your own time, but when it comes to being a productive member of society, that takes cooperation and subordination of personal concerns for the greater good of all.

A: In the long run, the greater good of all depends on achieving the greater good for each individual, and that is becoming a well-adjusted, self-accepting, emotionally stable person. If our educational system could do that, nothing else would be needed.

B: What about reading, writing, and arithmetic? And what about producing doctors, lawyers, teachers, and all the educated persons required for our high-tech workforce? Be realistic, life is not always just being yourself. Each of us has to be something society needs. Schools are society's instruments for providing primarily for society's needs and only secondarily for the needs of individuals.

What do you think? What is the first obligation of the schools and their teachers, to the individual or to society? Are the views of A and B necessarily incompatible? Can both societal and individual needs be met at the same time, or is some subordination of one to the other always necessary?

Curing Shyness

Jill Yablonski was concerned about Tom, a student in her fourth-grade class. Tom was one of those shy children who always seemed to be on the fringe of things. At recess, he usually played by himself. In class, he preferred to sit quietly and listen. He did not initiate exchanges with other students or with Jill. It was not that Tom was sullen. In fact, he was a pleasant child; it was just that he liked to keep to himself. His school work was good. The other children did not dislike him particularly, although they rarely associated with him. In short, Tom did not seem to be suffering from his shyness. His previous teachers all said that Tom had always been shy but had done well for them. But Jill was not satisfied with this. She thought Tom had just been ignored. Jill thought she ought to do something to help Tom learn to interact with other people.

She set about getting Tom involved. She got other children to play with him. She had Tom lead class discussions. Tom acquiesced in these activities without comment, and he seemed to handle them pretty well. Jill hoped this meant Tom was making progress.

Thus she was rather surprised when she received a note from Tom's parents, who said that Tom had become very unhappy about school. Where before Tom had always been eager to tell his day's experiences, lately he came close to tears and was unwilling to talk when asked about school. Tom's parents asked whether Jill had any idea what the problem was.

Jill did have an idea. She suspected that her program of personal growth and socialization was at the root of the matter. She was disturbed that Tom was unhappy; he had seemed to do well. She was not at all sure she should desist, though. It might be difficult in the short-term, but considered in a larger perspective, Tom ought to get over his shyness. It would be a handicap later. On the other hand, maybe she was pushing things. Maybe Tom would grow out of it on his own. Maybe he was simply a shy person.

What should Jill do? Should she change her approach? Is she correct in her diagnosis of Tom? Does taking a therapist approach to teaching mean leading a child to a goal perceived by the teacher as growth? Or does it mean permitting the child to grow in his own way? Does Jill have the right to make Tom unhappy for "his own good"? When, if ever, is intrusion in the personal development of others justified?

What Standard Shall We Use?

The faculty of Craigsdale High School is in an uproar. Susan Salerno, a new member of the faculty, has been raising questions at faculty meetings that strike at many long-held assumptions about the aims and policies of education. It all revolves around her grading policy. Susan believes that it is not fair to use a single standard of evaluation to grade all students in a class regardless of ability or level at which they begin. Such a system, she says, is not pedagogically tenable. Education aims at the growth of persons and must necessarily start at whatever level the student is at and reflect what that person is capable of achieving. A single standard against which all are graded is an externally imposed criterion that cannot measure personal growth. Further, such a standard distinguishes those who succeed from those who fail by creating failure even when a student may be doing his or her best. This system is especially untenable now that classes at Craigsdale are increasingly heterogeneous but cannot be justified even if that were not the case.

Early in the term, Susan asked her students to do a project. After giving them a grade for it and copious comments and suggestions for improvements, she had them redo the project for the end of the term. Students were then graded on how much they had improved from their first project. A student going from failing work to a C may get an *A* for the course. This procedure, Susan believes, more fairly evaluates student achievement and more adequately reflects what they have *learned*.

Susan's colleagues are not convinced. One of them, Tom Abelson, argues that education has traditionally been involved with setting standards of excellence for students to aspire to. Such standards are public measures of competence, and all students should be accountable to them. Ellen Myers adds that schools are expected to grade according to such a uniform standard. A system like Susan's throws into doubt the value of students' grades when they compete for scholarships or apply to schools of higher learning.

Susan replies to Tom that she *is* using a standard of excellence to assess student achievement. She evaluates their projects according to rigorous standards of excellence. However, when it comes to evaluating the *progress* students have made over the semester, she believes that they can only be their own measure of achievement.

To Ellen, Susan responds that it is unfortunate that the educational system is organized to a large extent the way she describes. However, that is no reason for continuing to use a policy that is pedagogically unjustified—in essence, having students compete according to a standard that may be inappropriate for them. Education should be about each person growing according to his or her own needs and abilities. Besides, grades often reflect the evaluation systems of individual teachers and are not comparable from school to school.

The case is not closed. What would you add to the continuing dialogue at Craigsdale? (Role playing might be useful here.) Does Susan have a point about the personal progress aspect of education? Is it fair or educative to evaluate students using a uniform standard of achievement? On the other hand, can we ignore public measures of educational success or failure? Should there be standards by which all are graded? What do you think?

Teaching "Relevant" Literature

Today had been a big day for Jennifer Calhoun. For the first time as a student teacher she had taken over the junior literature classes in which she had been observing. Jennifer had put a great deal of thought into the unit on twentieth-century American literature she was to teach for the next six weeks. The progressive theorists she had been reading about in her foundation course at State College greatly influenced her thinking, so she aimed to make the students themselves the center of her unit. She was not so concerned that the students learn to analyze literature; she wanted them to be excited by their work, enjoy their readings, and take away something meaningful from the class. In Jennifer's opinion, these things had not happened in the class up to that time.

So Jennifer spent a great deal of time developing a reading list that would be appealing and relevant to the students. She chose stories, poems, and books about teenagers, and some were even written by young people. Because the student population was diverse, she chose works by authors of different ethnic and racial backgrounds, too. The activities she developed concentrated on free discussion and creative writing assignments. She really wanted the students to become engaged with literature in a way that would help them to see themselves and to develop as persons; she structured her curriculum accordingly.

Armed with her enthusiasm and thoughtfully developed plan for meeting her goals, Jennifer introduced her unit to the classes (and to her supervisor, who was observing that day). But against her expectations, the students did not seem to be particularly excited by the readings and activities that Jennifer presented. Some even objected to them.

That afternoon, when discussing the day with her supervisor, Jennifer frankly admitted that she was puzzled and dejected by the students' reactions to her unit. The advice her supervisor offered puzzled Jennifer even more.

Her supervisor told her that by this time students were pretty set in their ways and new approaches were perceived as threatening. Also, in this junior class, many students were looking to apply to colleges. They knew that PSATs, SATs, and achievement tests were right around the corner and that standard questions on the literature sections would not be about the books on Jennifer's list. The supervisor advised Jennifer to return to the standard curriculum and standard assignments and tests. It was only fair to her students not to change things.

What would you do if you were Jennifer? Can and should the system and situational realities restrict the degree of freedom a teacher has in choosing an approach? What do you think?

Teacher and Mother?

Susie Simon was a new fifth-grader in Westville Elementary School. Eight months before, Susie's mother had been killed in a traffic accident. Susie's father was concerned that Susie needed the attention of female adults. Susie missed her mother very much, and Mr. Simon felt that he was unable to fill the roles of both father and mother. For that reason, when he enrolled Susie in Westville, he asked that she be placed in Michelle Saint Martin's class rather than in that of Mike Walsh, the other fifth-grade teacher. The principal assented to the request.

When Michelle met with her principal, he explained Mr. Simon's request. Susie needed a female role model, he said. She needed a woman to talk to and to listen to her problems. She needed affection.

Michelle listened with sympathy, but she was uneasy. She was not sure she could, or should, take on this responsibility. She had thirty-one other students in her class. Her time and energy were already extended to the limit. She could not see how she would be able to give Susie the individual attention she needed. Besides, Michelle just was not a "huggy" sort of person. Other teachers felt comfortable with overtly showing affection; but not Michelle. That was not her temperament. Anyway, she did not believe such relationships were in a student's best interests. Sure, her colleagues chided her for being too straight-laced, but none doubted her skill and commitment to teaching. Weren't those the important things, after all?

Michelle wished she could help Susie. But she was not sure the principal's way was the right way. She could be a good teacher for Susie, but she could not replace her mother. Michelle had the feeling that trying to force herself to be somebody she wasn't would be hypocritical and might lead to resentment. She did not want to do anything to harm Susie. What should she do?

Is parenting a proper component of teaching? Is the principal putting unreasonable demands on Michelle by asking her to change her approach in this case? Should she try to show more affection in her teaching? Are there ways to show it without making undue emotional or physical demands? What can be done to serve the best interests of Susie and the other students? What would you do if you were in Michelle's place?

Freedom and Indoctrination

A: We all grow up in the narrow world of our parents and friends, a small place where their views, beliefs, and values become ours through the process sociologists call primary socialization. Education gives us the opportunity to free ourselves from the accident of our birth in a particular time, place, and family. It broadens our horizons and helps us to become members of the family of man.

B: But there are many families of man. There are different nations and

different cultures, and that means education can't help but be indoctrination into one's national or cultural frame of mind. You may
escape the narrow confines of the family you are born into through
schooling, but you just trade that in for a narrow nationalistic or
cultural bias. No mind can really be free. Education is a form of
indoctrination.

A: Indoctrination means being taught things as if they were unquestion-
ably true. In America, we teach people that it's all right to question, to
challenge authority on logical, moral, or other reasonable grounds.
Freedom is not only being allowed to do that; in a democracy it is also
learning the skills needed to do it well. Learning to be a critical
thinker is what a liberal education should be about. Then we ourselves can determine truth and falsity, good and evil, and not behave
like unthinking sheep in a herd.

B: But a critical thinker can challenge everything and anything, right?
Then even the idea of a liberal education can be challenged! And what
about traditional values, beliefs, and norms? Isn't anything sacred or
just plain worth not challenging because it is appreciated, it is valued,
it is "our way"? Must everything be either true or false, right or
wrong when challenged by the critical thinker? Like Atlas holding up
the world on his shoulders, you have to be able to stand on something.

A: That something is our belief in reason, in having good evidence for
our claims, in open-mindedness, and in critical thinking.

B: But aren't those ideas just part of the Western liberal culture as it
evolved over the last three-hundred years? Other cultures believe in
authority and tradition, in group solidarity rather than rugged indi-
vidualism. Besides, even our so-called forms of knowledge are based
on conceptualizations of experience that are culture-laden. There's
no way for a mind, initiated into the knowledge base of a culture, to
be free.

What do you think? Is a liberationist approach to teaching possible?
Can a person learn to overcome cultural biases? To what extent can
education free the mind and to what extent must education be indoctrination?

Too Young to Be Critical?

Li Nguyen had some definite ideas about the aims of his junior high
social studies class. He wanted his students to be politically aware and
able to free themselves from the domination of political sloganeering.

Li proposed to accomplish this through critical inquiry in the social studies. In his class, the emphasis was on giving reasons for beliefs. Unsubstantiated claims were subjected to criticism. Critical, reasoned thought was the theme of his teaching.

Li was beginning to think his class was really achieving his aim when he was called into the principal's office. The principal told Li that she had received several complaints from parents that their children had come home advocating provocative and objectionable opinions on political and social issues. This situation was unsatisfactory to the parents not only because of the content of their children's opinions but because of the way they were held. Several of the parents complained that the children would not listen to them when they gave counterarguments. The children said that Mr. Nguyen told them they had a right to their own opinions in these matters. The parents demanded immediate change. Some had gone so far as to imply that, because of his background as a political refugee, Li was not motivated by scholarship but by self-serving concerns.

The principal asked Li to meet later with her and a few of the parents in order to explain his program. Li went back to his room to consider the principal's news. He resented the implication that he was selfishly motivated. But how was he to justify his approach? He was not sure that the situation was a bad one. He felt that perhaps rebellion was a necessary first step toward critical thinking. And he believed that children *did* have a right to question accepted beliefs. On the other hand, he was disturbed that some students were unwilling to listen to their parents' arguments. He had stressed the value of an open mind. Class discussions had emphasized the need to listen to others and give good reasons for one's own beliefs. The students had seemed to learn that lesson. What should Li do? What would you say to the parents if you were Li?

Are there ages where a liberationist approach might be inappropriate? If so, is the problem in the manner generally, or can a valid liberationist approach still be developed for any age group? Irrespective of age, to what extent is a liberationist approach appropriate for teaching if it brings a community's values into question?

Education for Life

P: If we have learned anything from the past, it's that we cannot predict the future. Before the twentieth century, atom splitting was considered impossible, and no one could possibly have anticipated the problems of nuclear waste or nuclear war. Therefore, educators cannot be content to teach what we think we now know. We must prepare people for the future by teaching them how to think and how to solve problems.

T: Problem solving is important, of course, and the future can't be known, that's true. But I believe that the best way to be prepared to face the future is with a rich knowledge of what human beings have come to know about themselves and their world and not just with some skills of critical thinking. In fact, critical thinking is best taught through a study of science, philosophy, and even art. These critical ways of thinking that are imbedded in our cultural heritage must be passed on by learning these subjects.

P: No, critical thinking and problem-solving skills are best learned, not through books and lectures on traditional subjects, but through experimentation and successful adaptations in real-life situations. Too much of schooling is a pedantic worshipping of traditions removed from the real world. No wonder students see little connection between life and what they learn in school. We must make learning meaningful, and that can only happen if people are not forced to study things disconnected from their lives but are given the opportunity to study what interests them.

T: But students are too young to know what's meaningful. We adults are better judges of what will be the rich rewards of a solid classical education. Interests can be fickle in youth. What's relevant today may not be so tomorrow. The wisdom of the past is always relevant.

P: Let's get down to brass tacks! What butcher or barber needs to know algebra or physics? What policeman, Shakespeare, or nurse, philosophy? What ordinary people need to know is how to solve *real* problems, how to be good workers, good parents, and good citizens. Your education is for an elite, not for good, ordinary people.

T: You are so short sighted! Good and productive lives are lived by people who are enriched by their education and not just taught how to do this or that. You would give people less than they deserve in the name of practical utility. I offer them their share of their rich cultural inheritance.

How do you react to this debate? Can critical thinking and problem-solving skills be taught apart from the liberal arts and sciences? Is a traditional curriculum the best preparation for life? Does a liberationist approach require both certain subject matters and certain skills? What do you think?

Freedom of Speech?

Joan Wagner has taught American history and government at Ringwood High School for fifteen years. Her students and colleagues consider Joan to be a fair and popular teacher. In her classroom she encourages her students to voice their opinions and to keep open minds. She insists that each student receive a fair hearing from the other students. On her part, Joan feels that it is important that she not impose her opinion on her students. It would be too easy, and unfair, to push her point of view successfully, taking advantage of her popularity and position of authority. Moreover, she would not want to humiliate students who have expressed different points of view. But most importantly, Joan would not impose her opinion because that would run counter to her goals as a teacher—to foster students' critical capabilities and to encourage them to participate in our democratic system of government.

Tommy Jones comes to class one day with a swastika drawn on his arm and a KKK leaflet taped to his notebook. Joan does not notice at first, but her attention is drawn to them during the course of the day because a black boy, Steven, and a Jewish girl, Rachel, approach him individually about them. Being the only black and the only Jew in the class, they are each too self-conscious to make an issue of them. Joan decides she has to talk to Tommy.

Joan has Tommy meet her after class the next day. Tommy is still sporting his swastika and KKK leaflet and makes it abundantly clear that he knows what the swastika and the KKK represent. In fact, he has read some literature, attended a KKK meeting, and thought the matter through carefully. He has decided that white Americans must protect themselves against Jews and blacks.

When Joan asks Tommy, please, not to come to class with such symbols, he asserts that he has freedom of speech and that he is merely expressing an informed opinion, as Joan has urged her students to do. Tommy says that he does not intend to get violent with Steven or Rachel. In response to Joan's suggestion that the beliefs of the Nazis and the KKK are offensive and threatening to Steven and Rachel even if he does not intend to hurt them physically, Tommy replies that the beliefs of blacks and Jews are threatening to white Christian Americans. Moreover, people have pro-abortion and antinuclear stickers on their notebooks. Would Joan ask those students not to come to class with those stickers because they are offensive to Tommy?

The next day, Tommy comes to class with the swastika and the leaflet in place. Joan later hears from a counselor that Steven's and Rachel's parents have suggested that they will have their children switch classes if nothing is done.

Should Joan insist that Tommy not come to class with the swastika and KKK leaflet? Should she defend Tommy's freedom of speech and suggest that Rachel's and Steven's parents likewise can exercise their freedom by switching their children's classes? Should Joan stand by while Tommy learns that he can be victorious and powerful with his swastika, since he and others might know why Steven and Rachel have left the class? Can Joan impose her opinion without countering the rules of her class, abandoning her liberationist approach, and exposing a student to humiliation? Can she raise this issue like any other issue in class, not knowing what the outcome will be as well as forcing Steven and Rachel to defend themselves? What do you think?

Mass or Class Culture?

A: Everybody complains about school being separate from life, but nobody does anything about it! Students are forced to read Shakespeare when in real life no one needs to force them to read comics and racy novels. They're forced to listen to symphonies and opera when in real life rock and country music sing to them. Art isn't in museums, but all around them in advertising and in the design of useful and beautiful products. Even our modern artists, the soup-can and comic-strip painters, saw that! Why do we persist in trying to initiate students into an artificially esoteric culture when their own real culture is so rich and satisfying? Why not help them critically engage in their culture of the real world and have school make a difference in their lives?

B: Because Shakespeare, Beethoven, and Rembrandt do make a difference in the lives of all of us. They represent some of the heights human beings have achieved, and their works speak eloquently to universal human emotions and feelings in ways barely plumbed in the pop culture. Why use mediocre examples to teach aesthetic and humane sensitivity when models of excellence are there for the taking?

A: Because students won't take them! Because students feel that their art forms are not appreciated by us. In fact, we make them feel as if their genuinely felt appreciation for their literature, art, movies, and music is a low form of uncultured, adolescent emotionalism, a phase one might have to go through but should grow out of. We treat as trivial and meaningless what they take very seriously as meaningful, as reflecting their deepest-felt emotions and needs.

B: Emotions are not what culture and art forms are about. It is intellect in its highest form that creates culture. The business of the school is developing intellect, not pampering the emotions. Television provides all the emotion, base action, and nonintellectual stimulation students need and then some. We need to counterbalance such negative cultural forces.

A: Why negative? Why must what speaks to masses of good, hard-working, plain people be negative and what speaks to only a few who see themselves as an elite be positive? Our levels of intellectual ability may differ, but all humans share the same emotional capacities to feel love, anger, empathy, caring, and joy. Our curriculum should capitalize on this capacity and use the common art forms of everyday life to bridge the gap between school and life and teach our youth about the common humanity of all human beings.

B: You win. Let's get rid of all the literature books from the storeroom and library and replace them with comics and drugstore paperbacks in our English courses. Let's clean out those old-fashioned instruments and classical records from the music room and replace them with guitars, electronic sound enhancement paraphernalia, and the latest pop records. As for art, let's . . .

A: Wait a minute, we don't have to go that far, do we?

What do you think? Does popular culture have a place in the curriculum? Does teaching high culture make students feel that their culture is inferior? Is it? Is the liberationist approach elitist?

Learning Chemistry by Discussion

Mr. Tanaka's high school chemistry class had been studying how chemical elements and compounds have unique physical properties such as solubility and density. Most recently, the students had observed in experiments how compounds show characteristic melting and freezing points. When compounds were heated and the temperatures graphed in relation to time, the students discovered that plateaus occur as the compounds change physical state from solid to liquid and from liquid to gas, and that these plateaus occur at different temperatures for different substances.

Today, Mr. Tanaka presented a problem to his students. He explained that he had been filling a container with a colorless liquid before class and had been called away to receive a phone call. When he returned, he continued filling the container, but with a different colorless liquid that he had taken up by mistake. The container sat on his desk. Mr. Tanaka asked if anyone in the class could think of a way to separate the two liquids so that the accidental mixture would not have to be thrown out.

After good naturedly reprimanding Mr. Tanaka for making such a careless error, the class began to think about the problem. There followed a lively discussion.

Art: That's a hard problem. I can see how one could separate marbles, say, but those are big and easy to see. Molecules are too tiny to separate.

Bernice: Maybe the liquids will separate themselves, like oil and water do.

Mr. Tanaka: Not a bad idea, Bernice. That's a technique that might work sometimes. Unfortunately, these chemicals mix completely.

Conrad: I don't know how this might work, but we've learned how molecules of different compounds behave differently. Could we use that fact somehow?

Dawn: I think Conrad is on to something there. Maybe we can't pick out molecules like marbles, but there could be some way that we could make the molecules sort themselves out.

Edgar: That's right. Like when we used filters to separate precipitates from liquids.

Mr. Tanaka: You've given some good ideas! There are filtering-like techniques, called chromatography, which can be used to separate liquids. We'll discuss that later. Can anyone think of other ways to make molecules separate themselves?

Fran: Compounds are different in how they respond to heating. Can we use that?

Mr. Tanaka: What do the rest of you think? What have we learned about heating compounds?

Grace: Well, we know that there are plateaus in the temperature-time graph where the compound changes its physical state. And different compounds have different freezing and boiling points.

Hector: I have an idea! If we heat the mixture, would one compound boil off first?

Ingrid: But how could you catch the gas that was boiled off?

Julio: What happens to the boiling points when compounds are mixed, though? Wouldn't the mixture have its own boiling point?

Mr. Tanaka: I'm pleased that you all have learned so much! Ingrid and Julio, you've raised some important problems we have to think about, but Hector is on the right track. We *can* use the difference in boiling points of some compounds to separate them when they are mixed.

This isn't always easy, for there are complications, just as Ingrid and Julio have suggested. This process of separation is called *distillation*, which, coincidentally, we will study next week.

Do you agree with Mr. Tanaka that the class had learned much, even though they raised many unanswered questions? How much, if anything, has the class learned about distillation as a result of the discussion? Did the students merely learn to attach a name to a process they already knew? Or did they learn something more? How would you characterize Mr. Tanaka's manner during this lesson? Was Mr. Tanaka's teaching strategy a good one? Would it be more efficient to teach about distillation more directly? Why or why not?

Different Learning Styles

The students in Ahmad Ali's sixth-grade class seemed to fall into three groups: those who liked a great deal of teacher attention and guidance, those who worked best independently, and those who fell in between, wanting some guidance but basically self-directed.

Because of this diversity, Ahmad sometimes found it difficult to meet the needs of all his students. This problem was particularly acute for science lessons. Ahmad liked to have his students do experiments and other hands-on science activities. But equipment and materials were limited, so it was usually necessary to divide the class into small groups so that each could work through an experiment while Ahmad engaged the larger groups in other activities. This arrangement did not sit well with the independent workers, nor with those who liked Ahmad's direct guidance, however. But Ahmad justified his plan to himself on the basis of the scarcity of equipment and the need for students to learn to work together. He considered this a necessary social skill. He also believed that doing experiments was a good way to learn science. Thus, he continued the small groups while taking care to be sure each contained a mixture of students with the three learning styles.

Still, he always had nagging doubts. While his students did well in science by and large, Ahmad was not sure he was being fair to the students who really preferred different arrangements. He wondered whether, if he put more thought and energy into the science lessons, he could find a way to deal better with all three learning styles and perhaps integrate different approaches into his teaching.

What would you do? What should decide one's teaching procedures and approach? Is it what students are comfortable with? What materials or equipment are available? What the teacher thinks ought to be done ideally? Is it possible to meet all students' needs? Should the teacher try to do that, or should all students learn to work together? What factors go into decisions about one's approach to teaching in a concrete situation like this?

Compatibility of Approaches

A: In their everyday teaching, teachers ordinarily use a variety of approaches depending on who and what they are teaching. In fact, a teacher might even use a variety of approaches in the same lesson.

B: I might be able to agree with you up to a point. But we need to be careful and not overestimate the compatibility of logically different approaches to teaching. For instance, if one is a liberationist teacher, one would rarely, if ever, act as an executive who dictates the what, when, and how of learning. And a therapist-type teacher certainly wouldn't do that either. Most teachers are quite consistent with their basic approach.

A: But you're talking as if teachers should pick one approach and stick to it no matter what, that to deviate from it would be inconsistent and unfaithful to their basic beliefs. But I'm suggesting that teachers don't need to choose one approach. They should be practical, not idealistic. Practicality calls for matching one's approach to the situation.

B: That's not practicality, that's ducking the issue. "How should I teach?" is the most fundamental professional question a teacher can ask and must answer for himself or herself. You have to care about and believe deeply in why you're doing what you do as a teacher or else you're just acting like a robot responding with built-in external programming to the contingencies of specific situations.

A: But you need not be a robot. A teacher can really believe in the value of each approach and use each intelligently as different situations demand.

B: That sounds good in theory, but I don't think it's possible in practice. It would be like saying one can be a Christian sometimes, a Moslem sometimes, and a Jew sometimes, depending on the spiritual situation. Approaches to teaching are more like religious faiths than like hats you can put on and take off at will. They require a fundamental commitment to deeply believed views about the purpose and value of education in the lives of human beings.

A: Yes, there is that philosophical quality to the calling of teaching, but I still think a good person, a committed teacher, can believe in the use of technical proficiency in aiming both at a student's personal growth and at a depth of knowledge in the traditional subjects without being inconsistent.

B: Perhaps, but not without admitting to a failure to choose to be what one deeply believes in being as an educator.

C: I've been listening to you both and I can't believe what I hear. Choice, approach, religion, philosophy. . . ? Teaching is just a job like any other. You do the best you can, given the social, political, and local realities that you find yourself in. Whatever you might decide or commit yourself to beforehand won't make any difference once you see all the constraints of your job. All this soul searching is just wasted effort. Just learn how to do it and do it. That's all the people want of you.

What do you think? Whose side are you on in this dispute? Why?

NOTES
BIBLIOGRAPHIC ESSAY

Notes

Chapter 1

1. Another version of the liberationist approach has recently emerged from contemporary neo-Marxist thought, which aims to emancipate ordinary people from the economic and political forces in society that hold them back and keep them from full equality. We have treated this version of the liberationist approach as emancipation in other books in this series. If it is of concern to you, you should read about it there. See Walter Feinberg and Jonas F. Soltis, *School and Society* (New York: Teachers College Press, 1985); and Decker F. Walker and Jonas F. Soltis, *Curriculum and Aims* (New York: Teachers College Press, 1986). Black studies and women's studies provide two examples of the purpose of the emancipation-liberationist approach, which is to raise consciousness regarding the biases and stereotypical thinking that have held back these groups in our society. The emancipator believes that freedom only comes by ridding ourselves of "false consciousness," of ways of perceiving the world that enslave us and others.

Chapter 2

1. David C. Berliner, "The Executive Functions of Teaching," *Instructor*, September 1983: 29–39.

2. The best description of this study for the practicing educator is Carolyn Denham and Ann Lieberman, eds., *Time to Learn* (Washington, D.C.: National Institute of Education, 1980).

3. Thomas L. Good, "Teacher Effectiveness in the Elementary School," *Journal of Teacher Education*, March-April 1979: 53.

4. B. F. Skinner, *The Technology of Teaching* (New York: Appleton-Century-Crofts, 1968), p. 21.

5. Ibid., p. 64.

6. James S. Coleman et al., *Equality of Educational Opportunity* (Washington, D.C.: United States Government Printing Office, 1966).

7. Thomas L. Good, Bruce J. Biddle, and Jere E. Brophy, *Teachers Make a Difference* (New York: Holt, Rinehart and Winston, 1975).

Chapter 3

1. Paul Goodman, *Growing Up Absurd* (New York: Random House, 1956).
2. Paul Goodman, *Compulsory Mis-Education* (New York: Horizon Press, 1964).
3. Paul Goodman, "Freedom and Learning: The Need for Choice," *Saturday Review*, May 18, 1968: 73.
4. Ibid.
5. Ibid.
6. Herbert Kohl, *36 Children* (New York: Signet, New American Library, 1967), pp. 25–26.
7. Abraham Maslow, *Toward a Psychology of Being* (New York: Van Nostrand, 1962).
8. Carl Rogers, *Freedom to Learn* (Columbus, O.: Charles E. Merrill, 1969), p. 103.
9. Ibid., p. 125.
10. Ibid., p. 152.
11. Ibid., p. 153.
12. Ibid.
13. Ibid., p. 108.
14. Jean-Paul Sartre, "Existentialism Is a Humanism," in Walter Kaufmann, ed., *Existentialism from Dostoevsky to Sartre* (Cleveland, O.: Meridian/World Publishing, 1956), pp. 290–291.
15. Walter Kaufmann, "Chapter 1: Existentialism from Dostoevsky to Sartre," in Kaufmann, ed., *Existentialism from Dostoevsky to Sartre*, p. 51.

Chapter 4

1. R. S. Peters, "Aims of Education—A Conceptual Inquiry," in R. S. Peters, ed., *The Philosophy of Education* (London: Oxford University Press, 1973), p. 25.
2. Gilbert Ryle, "Can Virtue Be Taught?" in R. F. Dearden, P. H. Hirst, and R. S. Peters, eds., *Education and Reason: Part 3 of Education and the Development of Reason* (London: Routledge & Kegan Paul, 1975), p. 47.
3. Urie Bronfenbrenner, *Two Worlds of Childhood: U.S. and U.S.S.R.* (New York: Simon and Schuster, 1970; Clarion paperback, 1972), quotation from p. 117 of paperback edition.
4. P. H. Hirst, "Liberal Education and the Nature of Knowledge," in Peters, ed., *The Philosophy of Education*, pp. 87–111; also in Dearden, Hirst, and Peters, eds., *Education and Reason: Part 3*, pp. 1–24.
5. Jerome S. Bruner, *The Process of Education* (Cambridge, Mass.: Harvard University Press, 1960; New York: Random House Vintage Edition, 1963), quotation from p. 71 of the Vintage edition.
6. Ibid. (Vintage edition), pp. 12–13.
7. Ibid., p. 12.

8. Mortimer J. Adler, *The Paideia Proposal: An Educational Manifesto* (New York: Macmillan, 1982), pp. 19–20.

9. Ibid., p. 20.

10. Jane Roland Martin, "Needed: A New Paradigm for Liberal Education," in Jonas F. Soltis, ed., *Philosophy and Education: Eightieth Yearbook of the National Society for the Study of Education* (Chicago: University of Chicago Press, 1981), p. 44.

Chapter 5

1. Harry S. Broudy, *The Real World of Public Schools* (New York: Harcourt Brace Jovanovich, 1972), p. 82.

2. Maxine Greene, *Teacher as Stranger* (Belmont, Calif.: Wadsworth, 1973), p. 286.

Bibliographic Essay

The Executive Approach

The notion of the executive functions of teaching was developed by one of the most eminent of contemporary researchers on teaching, David C. Berliner. Berliner directed the groundbreaking study, the Beginning Teacher Evaluation Study. The best description of this study for the practicing educator is edited by Carolyn Denham and Ann Lieberman, *Time to Learn* (Washington, D.C.: National Institute of Education, 1980). For a more recent treatment, and one that includes the classic analysis of instructional time by John Carroll, see Charles W. Fisher and David C. Berliner (eds.), *Perspectives on Instructional Time* (New York: Longman, 1985). The notion of the teacher as executive is developed in David C. Berliner, "The Executive Functions of Teaching," *Instructor*, September 1983: 29–39. The 1979 piece by Thomas L. Good, "Teacher Effectiveness in the Elementary School," summarizes a good bit of the research to that time; it appeared in the *Journal of Teacher Education*, March-April 1979: 52–64. Good also collaborated with Bruce J. Biddle and Jere E. Brophy on *Teachers Make a Difference* (New York: Holt, Rinehart and Winston, 1975). The quotations from B. F. Skinner in chapter 2 are taken from *The Technology of Teaching* (New York: Appleton-Century-Crofts, 1968), an excellent collection of Skinner's articles dealing with education, particularly his pioneering work on teaching machines. The Coleman Report, *Equality of Educational Opportunity*, was published by the United States Government Printing Office in 1966. Anyone wishing to comprehend its impact on education over the subsequent six years would enjoy reading Godfrey Hodgson's "Do Schools Make a Difference?" *The Atlantic*, March 1973: 35–46.

If you are beginning a career as a teacher and would like a practical guide to the executive approach to teaching, a booklet published by the American Association of School Administrators entitled *Time on Task* (1982) is one of the best short, applied pieces available to date. A more extensive and academic, but quite comprehensible, treatment is N. L.

Gage, *The Scientific Basis of the Art of Teaching* (New York: Teachers College Press, 1978). Gage probably has the best claim to being the father of the modern research-on-teaching movement. His seminal piece in this area appears in the first *Handbook of Research on Teaching*, which he edited for Rand McNally (Chicago, 1963). Gage's most recent statement is an argument for the power of recent advances in research on teaching; it is entitled *Hard Gains in the Soft Sciences* (Bloomington, Ill.: Phi Delta Kappa, 1985). An extensive treatment of recent research on many topics of vital interest to educators will be forthcoming; it is *The Educator's Handbook: Research into Practice*, edited by Virginia Richardson Koehler (New York: Longman, in press). Finally, the most up-to-date work for scholars in this area will appear in the third edition of the *Handbook of Research on Teaching*, edited by Merlin C. Wittrock, and scheduled for publication by Macmillan in 1986.

The Therapist Approach

If you have an interest in recent history, the so-called popular reform books of the sixties are fascinating to read and extremely provocative. Among the best in education are the following: George Dennison, *The Lives of Children* (New York: Vintage/Random House, 1969); Herbert Kohl, *36 Children* (New York: Signet, New American Library, 1967); Jonathan Kozol, *Death at an Early Age* (New York: Houghton Mifflin, 1967); Ivan Illich, *Deschooling Society* (New York: Harper & Row, 1970); A. S. Neill, *Summerhill* (New York: Hart Publishing, 1960); and Everett Reimer, *School Is Dead* (Garden City, N.Y.: Doubleday Anchor, 1971). The work of Paul Goodman is, of course, now classic. *Growing Up Absurd* was published by Random House in 1956. The Goodman quotations in chapter 3 were taken from an excellent short piece called "Freedom and Learning: The Need for Choice," which he wrote for the *Saturday Review* (May 18, 1968, pp. 73–75).

There are many works on humanistic psychology. One of the best introductions for the beginner is a short anthology edited by Floyd W. Matson, *Without/Within: Behaviorism and Humanism* (Belmont, Calif.: Wadsworth, 1973). There is no reason to avoid the original works, however. They are well written and filled with appealing ideas. See especially the pivotal work: Carl R. Rogers, *Freedom to Learn* (Columbus, O.: Charles E. Merrill, 1969). Also vitally important are Gordon W. Allport, *Becoming* (New Haven, Conn.: Yale University Press, 1955), and Abraham H. Maslow, *Toward a Psychology of Being* (New York: Van Nostrand, 1962).

It is somewhat more difficult to recommend works on existentialism to the beginning teacher. There are different types of existentialists—literary, philosophical, religious—and none of them wrote very directly about education. Perhaps the most accessible general introduction would be David Denton (ed.), *Existentialism and Phenomenology in Education* (New York: Teachers College Press, 1974). If you wish to get a sense of what an existential commitment means in teaching, one of the best works you can read is Maxine Greene's *Teacher as Stranger* (Belmont, Calif.: Wadsworth, 1973). Existentialist writing is generally not easy to follow. It sometimes helps to become familiar with several different views before becoming deeply enmeshed in a particular version or writer. The edited selections in Walter Kaufmann's *Existentialism from Dostoevsky to Sartre* (Cleveland, O.: Meridian/World Publishing, 1956) are choice pieces by many of the best existentialist writers. An excellent set of papers examining the classic work in existentialism is contained in George Alfred Schrader, Jr. (ed.), *Existential Philosophers: Kierkegaard to Merleau-Ponty* (New York: McGraw-Hill, 1967). Schrader also provides a very helpful introduction.

The Liberationist Approach

There is an enormous literature on what we have called the liberationist approach to teaching, primarily because this approach has deep historical roots and is so closely connected to philosophical ideas. Any text that spans the history of education from ancient to modern times will suggest a host of important sources to read. One that we find ourselves turning to again and again is Kingsley Price, *Education and Philosophical Thought*, 2d ed. (Boston: Allyn and Bacon, 1967). As for some of the more recent work, it may be helpful to begin with what might be called the inspirational literature in liberal education, meaning that it is intended to offer the reader encouragement to emulate the great achievements of humankind. Gilbert Highet has written two such pieces that are exceptional examples of the genre: *Man's Unconquerable Mind* (New York: Columbia University Press, 1954) and *The Immortal Profession* (New York: Weybright and Talley, 1976). Mortimer J. Adler's *The Paideia Proposal: An Educational Manifesto* (New York: Macmillan, 1982), discussed in chapter 4, is a brief, highly readable argument for liberal education in today's schools.

As the reader enters the more strictly philosophical literature, the complexity increases a bit, but so does the depth of understanding. The work of the British philosophers R. S. Peters and P. H. Hirst is widely available. Two key sources of their writing are identified in the notes to chapter 4. Another excellent treatment is John Passmore's *The Philosophy of Teaching* (Cambridge, Mass.: Harvard University Press, 1980). Passmore attempts to explicate the emotional aspects of the liberationist approach with the same intensity as the knowledge aspects. Several American philosophers of education have propounded related views but with significant adaptations. One of these is D. Bob Gowin, whose *Educating* (Ithaca, N.Y.: Cornell University Press, 1981) brings a strong element of John Dewey (a leading American philosopher and educator whose seminal works spanned the first half of this century) to the liberationist approach. Thomas F. Green, another American philosopher who has formulated a strong liberationist view of education, sets forth an extended and powerful analysis of teaching in *The Activities of Teaching* (New York: McGraw-Hill, 1971).

Finally, if you would like to examine the psychological and ethical assumptions undergirding the liberationist approach, we do not hesitate to recommend the other books in the same series as this one. *Perspectives on Learning* by D. C. Phillips and Jonas F. Soltis examines several of the psychologies discussed in this book, and *The Ethics of Teaching* by Kenneth A. Strike and Jonas F. Soltis raises many of the ethical issues inherent in the several approaches to teaching. The chapters on Marxism, the hidden curriculum, and socialization in *School and Society* by Walter Feinberg and Jonas F. Soltis add a critical political and economic perspective to the liberationist approach to teaching. And *Curriculum and Aims* by Decker F. Walker and Jonas F. Soltis deals with issues concerning the purpose and content of education.